MW01235054

SURVIVE FOR PURPOSE

D. Samuel Gardayea Menyongar
with
Stanley Vinson Burdette

SURVIVE FOR PURPOSE

The magnificent autobiography and memoirs of survivor,
D. Samuel Gardayea Menyongar

Discovering the power of God in the midst of brutal civil wars in
Liberia and Sierra Leone . . .

Recalling the magnificent intervention of God on his behalf . . .

Telling the world the tragedy, mayhem, pain, adversity, hurt and
sorrows of those who cannot tell it themselves.

Friends, I want to submit to you that the people you associate with, the
books you read, the images you see on TV and in the movies and the
words you choose to listen to will determine what you will become in
the next weeks, months and years to come. Read this book and your
life will never be the same again.

"Out of the ashes of defeat burns the greatest fire of accomplishment."
–Thomas Edison

CONTENTS

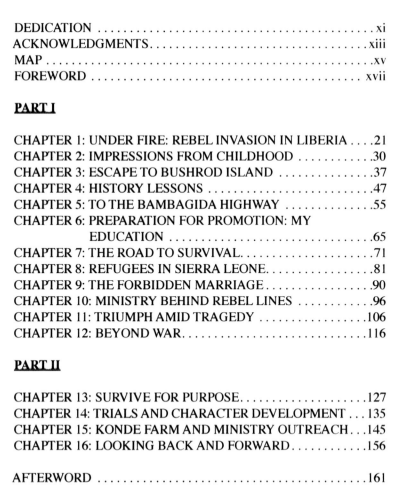

I first met Brother Samuel Menyongar in 1996 in Sierra Leone. We were both students together at a missionary training school. Shortly after finishing school, we began working directly together, and did so for many years, until 2014. I saw some of the events firsthand that Samuel mentioned in the book when I lived and worked in Sierra Leone from 1996-1998. There is only one way to explain Bro. Samuel's "test of survival"—God's faithfulness. Now, Brother Samuel will be facing perhaps an even greater "test of survival," the fame and recognition that come with publishing a bestselling book. I am convinced that the same God who kept him alive through a brutal civil war is the same God who can keep him from the attacks that fame sends his way. Proverbs 27:21,"Fire tests the purity of silver and gold, but a person is tested by being praised." Brother Samuel is a brother that I will always hold up in prayer.

Mark Stewart, President, Hope Universal

DEDICATION

I dedicate this book to my parents, Deacon and Mrs. Samuel Dee Menyongar, who taught me to love God and follow Him. I will never forget their love and support to me.

I also dedicate this book to my lovely wife, Mariama, and our wonderful children: Manasseh, Ephraimnelle (Rebekah), Rugiatu, Fatmata, and Joshua.

I also dedicate this book to all those who perished during the wars in Liberia from 1989–2003, to those who perished in Sierra Leone from 1991–2002, and to all the survivors.

ACKNOWLEDGMENTS

To God be all the glory for great things He has done. Everything we are and will become is only by the grace of God. Therefore, we must be grateful to our God at all times. If it had not been for the Lord on my side, where would I be? He has brought me too far and I cannot turn back. I thank God for the opportunity to write this book. I also thank the people who have contributed immensely to my life.

It is a privilege and honor to express gratitude to the following people:
- My parents, Mr. and Mrs. Samuel Dee Menyongar
- My uncle, Mr. Philip Weakon Menyongar
- Brother David Orr, Brother Russell Tatro
- Mr. and Mrs. Mark Stewart, President of Hope Universal
- Hope Universal Board Members: Pastor Joe Bacher, Mr. Vernon Bacher, Dorothy Hershberger, Ruth Hershberger, Drs. Vimala and Kunjappan John, Dr. Michael Kunkel, Mr. Larry Reeves, and Mr. Billy Stoll
- Hope Universal volunteers: Mr. Vinson Burdette, Jane Chupp, Tammy (Crooks) Drost, Mr. and Mrs. Reynolds Holiman, Mr. and Mrs. Kent McGahey, David Peachy, Mr. and Mrs. Greg Vieau, and Rachel Yoder
- The Word Made Flesh staff: Mr. and Mrs. Chris Heuertz
- All my fellow ministers, friends, and staff of the International Missionary Center: Bishop and Mrs. Darlingston G. Johnson, Rev. and Mrs. Julius Laggah, Mr. Winston Togba, and Rev. and Mrs. Emeric Webber

I also thank Jonathan and Katja Starkey who, after visiting Sierra Leone, helped tremendously to bring awareness to the American people about the atrocities committed against innocent people in Sierra Leone and Liberia during the years of war.

I appreciate the support and friendship of Mr. and Mrs. Michael Alley, Mr. and Mrs. Ron Cummings, Mr. and Mrs. John Drewes, Mr. and Mrs. Jimmy Duren, Mr. and Mrs. Alex Espinoza, Mr. And Mrs. Keith Padgett, Mr. and Mrs. John and Lori Robb, Mr. and Mrs. Geoff Severin, Dr. and Mrs. Richard Shaka.

MAP

Africa

FOREWORD

*The continent of Africa has given the world many of its
most glittering jewels, but these diamonds do not shine
when they are first discovered, they are only dull stones,
and must be cut and ground before they glow with the
colors of the rainbow.*

—Samuel Kaboo Morris

The quote above is taken from the biography of Samuel Kaboo Morris, a missionary from Liberia, who went to the USA in the 1870s. I read the biography of Morris in July 2004 on a flight from one of my trips to the USA. The quote above from Morris motivated me to put my experiences into writing.

At that time I was returning from Ontario, California, after speaking to a group of women known as the Women of Vision in a church called Hope Chapel. I had the opportunity to go on the beach at the Huntington State Beach on the Pacific Ocean, visit Universal Studio in Hollywood, and go to the Campus Crusade for Christ/Jesus Film project headquarters.

Later, I visited the USA again. I met with Joe Bacher in South Carolina. Joe is a missionary-pastor friend who has been to Sierra Leone and Liberia on missions trips several times from his home in Westminster, SC. After hearing my story Joe encouraged me to record it and suggested it be put in book form. Joe and his wife, Sister Cathy, and their children have been very supportive of me and my family since we first met in 2002.

As I sat on the plane on my return flight, I thought of the goodness of the Lord and how he has blessed me and my family. Therefore, it is important to me to put into writing the goodness of God in our lives for others to be able to read. Hopefully, my story will motivate others to know that God can turn them from zero to hero, from nothing to something, from least to greatest, from nobody to somebody. There is hope for everyone. The devil will have to let go. The best days of life can begin now.

PART I

CHAPTER ONE

UNDER FIRE: REBEL INVASION IN LIBERIA

I remember the weight of my clothes in a black plastic bag atop my head in the tropical heat of southwest Liberia as I followed my parents toward Cesstos. The memory remains vivid even though I was only four years old at the time. We faced a two-hour walk to Cesstos where we planned to catch a ride in the back of a pickup truck heading to Monrovia. I trudged ahead in bare feet on the warm ground, the rocky path retaining little trace of my footsteps.

I remember the image of my father holding the hand of my three-year-old brother as they walked ahead of me on that morning. Behind my father and brother, I walked between my mother and four sisters. Farther back were several men from our village who had volunteered to help us carry our belongings to Cesstos. We talked little as we walked under the green canopy of remote jungle separating us from our destination. My eyes occasionally followed the swinging path of brown monkeys moving through the trees. I recognized the sounds of the seemingly chanting dodo birds as they sang from their perches. Though sad to be leaving the village of my birth, I was excited to be traveling to the mysterious city called Monrovia.

After finally arriving in Cesstos we waited for several hours before boarding the truck that would carry us to Monrovia. My mother and father sat in the front of the truck. The six of us children were placed in the back of the truck on benches or in the lap of an older sibling. All of us were nervous. Except for my father and mother, we had never ridden in a vehicle.

We huddled together in the back of the truck along with other passengers, all of us facing our belongings piled in the center of the truck bed. For four hours we traveled in the noisy truck, stopping only for food, beverages, and bathroom breaks in the bush. I remember drinking soda for the first time during one of our stops. I can still remember the sweet taste of that first bottled soda. As we approached Buchanan, Liberia's second largest city, we children gazed in awe at the increased number of cars and trucks we saw on the mostly dirt roads we traveled. Each mile brought us closer to Monrovia, Liberia's capital city, where we would meet my uncle and my older brother.

Our long journey drew to a close as our dusty truck entered Monrovia after dark, its headlights blending in with the many other lights of the city. I was amazed at what I saw in Monrovia. Streetlights, tall buildings, paved streets with sidewalks, and vehicles traveling in all directions were amazing sights for my tired eyes. We drove on through the invisible sounds of music flowing out of shops and clubs.

Finally, much later than my normal bedtime, we arrived at our destination: a street near my father's house where my uncle and brother were. I remember the many people who crowded around the truck, welcoming us to our new home and helping us unload our belongings. I was excited to be in Monrovia. As we greeted our new neighbors, joy and laughter filled the air. Little did I know that years later the sounds of joy and laughter would be replaced by sounds of gunfire and fearful cries as war spilled into Monrovia.

By 1989, eighteen years after my family moved to Monrovia, televisions were scarce in that area. I remember occasionally seeing episodes of "Bonanza" or "Wild, Wild West" on a black and white TV at a house where we earned viewing time by washing floors, cutting grass, or sweeping the yard. The privilege of watching TV was a once-a-week treat at the most.

In December of 1989, many people gathered in excitement around a limited number of TVs to see the much anticipated series "V: the Final Battle," a show about an invasion of aliens. Following one episode, a newscaster appeared on screen, announcing that a group of men had crossed the border of neighboring Cote d'Ivoire (Ivory Coast) and attacked Liberia. Promising to give more details later, the news announcer stated that Liberia was at war.

Many factors contributed to the eruption of war. Before the civil war started, great hatred and animosity existed among various tribes. On one side were the Krahn and Sarpo tribes and on the other side were the Gio and Mano tribes. Roots of the hatred among those groups extended back hundreds of years. Both sets of tribes felt that they were superior and they tried to demonstrate their superiority by capturing, killing, and even eating members of the rival tribes. The ritual of eating the flesh of an enemy supposedly provided supernatural power to subdue them. Although ritualistic cannibalism had decreased in the 20th century, a critical event in 1985 changed contributed to a reemergence of the vile deed.

In 1985, Liberia's President, Samuel Doe, accused the head of the Armed Forces of Liberia (AFL) of plotting a coup against him. The accused head of the national military, Thomas Quiwonkpa, had been appointed by Doe himself shortly after becoming President in 1980. Quiwonkpa was a member of the Peoples Redemption Council (PRC) and had been instrumental in overthrowing former President William R. Tolbert, who led the country from 1971 until his assassination in 1980.

As a result, of Samuel Doe's suspicion of Quiwonkpa, those loyal to Doe captured and killed Quiwonkpa, a member of the Gio tribe. The killing of Quiwonkpa opened old wounds and stirred the animosity that had historically existed between the Krahn/Sapro tribes and the Gio/Mano tribes. Because Quiwonkpa was a Gio and Doe was a Krahn, the old lines of conflict were reignited. Adding to the hatred was the fact that Doe's men paraded around Monrovia showing off parts of the body of Quiwonkpa. That event in 1985 not only brought back old conflicts, but also the brutality and inhumanity of ritualistic killing, including cannibalism.

In 1987, another event occurred that fueled the animosity between the Krahn/Sapro and Gio/Mano tribes. In that year, soldiers in Doe's army went to Nimba County in southeast Liberia and massacred many men, women, and children who were members of the Gio and Mano tribes. The reason for the massacre was based in an accusation that men from Nimba County were planning to overthrow the government led by Doe. As a result of this massacre, most of the able-bodied men fled Nimba County and entered Cote d'Ivoire (Ivory Coast), Burkina Faso, and later made their way to Libya to receive military training.

The hatred and animosity grew until 1989 when the National Patriotic Front of Liberia (NPFL), headed by Charles Taylor, entered Liberia. Perhaps not coincidentally, Taylor and his rebel forces first made their presence known in Nimba County, which was mainly populated by members of the Gio/Mano tribes. Taylor and his forces quickly and violently eliminated the small number of Armed Forces of Liberia (AFL) soldiers who were stationed in Nimba County.

After the NPFL invaded and took control of Nimba County, members of the AFL loyal to Doe reacted strongly with violence of their own.

At that time, we read each day about multiple instances of beheadings of civilians in Monrovia. Published in newspapers in Monrovia were photographs of freshly removed heads, along with names of those who had been mercilessly killed. Widely known was the fact that the names of those beheaded and photographed were members of the Gio and Mano tribes.

Those acts of violence served as AFL retaliation for the invasion of Liberia by Taylor's forces. AFL soldiers hunted down members of the Gio and Mano tribal groups; anyone speaking the languages associated with those tribes were in peril. Under cover of the darkness of night, many were taken to beaches and executed. As a result, many members of the Gio and Mano tribes in and around Monrovia fled due to fear. Many of them fled to St. Peter Lutheran Church in Sinkor, Monrovia; they went to the church in hopes that it would be a safe place to gather.

As the NPFL rebels advanced closer to Monrovia, the Liberian Council of Churches (LCC) called all peace-loving Liberians and students to gather at the United Methodist Church headquarters on 12th Street of Monrovia. It was the third week in April 1990, and tens of thousands of people had gathered at this location; I know because I attended this rally. We held placards up, saying such things as, "WE ARE TIRED. LET THIS SENSELESS WAR END" and "INNOCENT PEOPLE ARE DYING. BRING THIS WAR TO AN END." We marched to the centennial pavilion, where the nation celebrated its hundred years of existence in 1947.

Liberian women demonstrating for war to end

24

At the centennial pavilion, those who were leading this march and rally led us in prayers for the nation. Some of those who prayed were the Bishop Arthur Kulah of the United Methodist Church, Rev. Momodu Diggs of the Providence Baptist Church, Bishop David Daniels of the Elizer Turner Memorial African Methodist Episcopal Church, Rev. Samuel Reeves and other ministers. After the time of prayer, the group marched up to Ashmun Street, on to Randall Street, and to the United Nations Drive. This route led to the Capitol building, which is the House of Parliament, where the group planned to present a petition to the legislators (senators and representatives) asking for the president to resign to avoid further bloodshed in the nation.

As we got between the central prison at South Beach and the Palm Grove cemetery, AFL soldiers came among the citizens who were peacefully marching and began to shoot—first in the air, and then at people. Many ran in all directions; from the midst of the stampede were cries of women and men running for their lives. I ran and fell between two houses, and many people walked over me, but I later managed to get up. My knees were seriously wounded, and my clothes were torn. That was a very bad sign, because I knew if I were to be seen, my injuries and torn clothing would identify me as one who had been marching.

I ran into a nearby house with many others I did not know and asked to hide with them. We looked through the windows of that house and saw soldiers arresting anyone they met on the road. The people were soaked because it had rained heavily. Then the soldiers started knocking on doors, looking for those hiding so they could arrest them. I knew if we were arrested, we would be grouped with the many others already been captured.

That day, we came near to death. Some AFL soldiers came to the house and knocked at the door. The landlady went to the door and opened it slowly. She told the soldiers that no one had entered the house. They believed her. Before the men came to this house, the landlady took us to hide under the bed. Under the bed we were afraid and praying, "O God, please do not allow them to see us or enter this house." We stayed in this house until we left at about 5:30 p.m. I had to remove my torn clothes and wore another's clothes to go back home after the AFL soldiers moved from that area.

The reason for the attack on the peaceful marchers was clear. The AFL had received instruction from Doe that if this group was successful in presenting the petition to the legislators, they would have the constitutional power to remove Doe from power. To avoid that prospect, Doe sent the military to disperse the crowd and arrest as many as they could and cause them to fear. It's true that the march was designed to be a peaceful political expression. Earlier, the LCC had asked Doe to step down. In response, Doe said that for the president to step down a majority of citizens should take a petition to the legislators and call for impeachment of the president. That rally was ended abruptly and violently. The citizens would not do anything again and many people were afraid they would be arrested or shot if they marched. For this reason many people watched with fear and apprehension as the tangled lines of conflict began to be established.

Day after day, more and more people came from the interior of the country and brought with them reports of the war. Tension in the city mounted. Adding to the stress were the horrible images in the newspapers of decapitated bodies. Some of the ministers in the government went to Ivory Coast and Sierra Leone to meet with the rebels for peace talks, but nothing good came out of those meetings and those ministers never came back. Some of them were Emmanuel Bowier the Minister of Information, Cultural Affairs and Tourism; Jenkins Scott, the Minister of Justice; and the first General who announced from Nimba County that the nation was at war left the country also. Most interpreted that action as a sign that there was no hope in the government and anything could happen.

By May 1990, conflict was imminent in the city of Monrovia. As the result of months of increased tensions, citizens were on edge and unsure what would happen or what to do. The reality of the conflict set in when people from northeast (Nimba County) and central (Bong County) fled to Monrovia. Crying in horror, women and children began streaming into the streets of Monrovia with accounts of invasion and atrocities. Few men made it to the city; most had been killed or forced to join the growing numbers of rebel forces. Discussions erupted about what the residents of Monrovia should do if—and when—the invasion of Monrovia occurred.

There were all kinds of stories told about the war that made it sound as if it was happening in a faraway land. It was not until more wounded soldiers of the AFL were brought from the war front and dead soldiers also were carried in military trucks that we began to see that it was actually taking place in our country. Families and displaced people who had walked hundreds of miles told how their relatives had been killed and houses burned, how pregnant women's wombs were cut open and the live babies were taken out and split into half and some of the rebels drank the blood. Moreover, others hearts were cut out and eaten—a worse form of cannibalism. Some Monrovians were sorry for the displaced people and gave them a place to stay. But other displaced individuals knew that the war would eventually come to Monrovia and refused to stay. They decided to move on and leave the country. Fear permeated the atmosphere in Monrovia.

Two things stand out in my mind about July 8, 1990. I remember Germany beating Argentina 1-0 in the World Cup soccer final at the Stadio Olimpico in Rome. Also, while at our home in Bassa Community, I remember a military man who lived in our neighborhood knocking at our door. It was curfew time. He shouted with excitement that we should come out and celebrate because Germany had won the World Cup. But we did not go outside because of the curfew. In addition to not wanting to break curfew, we also had in mind the rumors that had been circulating about a possible invasion of Monrovia. In addition to fear about a possible rebel invasion, we had heard that some remnant of Doe's AFL, was coming to invade our community—a point that requires some explanation.

It was well known by July 1990 that the rebels were "hitting and running" in outlying areas near Monrovia. In the town of Paynesville, a suburb east of Monrovia, rebels had attacked, killing civilians and conscripting young men into the rebel movement. Other military men had volunteered to join the rebel forces. Because of these events, some residents in Monrovia began meeting to pray for God's intervention concerning the war.

The number of people meeting to pray began to increase as news spread. Led by Rev. J. Edwin Lloyd, then President of the Liberia National Red Cross, the prayer meetings grew. As numbers increased the prayer meetings were held at the St. Simon Baptist Church facility, which was large enough to accommodate the crowds. As the prayer meetings continued, so too did the violence. Unfortunately, some members of the Armed Forces of Liberia who were loyal to Samuel Doe grew suspicious about the prayer meetings. Those loyal to Doe mistakenly thought that the prayers were offered against them, in hopes that they would be overthrown by the rebels.

On that memorable night of July 8, 1990, the military man who knocked on our door encouraging us to celebrate the World Cup victory was not one of those loyal to Doe. He innocently wanted others to join him in celebrating the German's victory. Later that night, however, the faction of the AFL loyal to Doe—those who had been suspicious of the prayer meetings—invaded our neighborhood in the Bassa Community of Monrovia.

First there was the sound of gunfire, automatic weapons shattering the stillness of the night. Then shouts and orders rang out as some buildings were surrounded and people were ordered to come outside. Through wooden windows red glints of bullets and the blazes from buildings on fire were visible. Throughout the night there was heavy shooting as sounds of gunfire mixed with screams and cries from confused individuals under attack.

Our house was made of concrete with timbers supporting a zinc (tin) roof. Although there were eleven rooms in the house, approximately thirty people lived there at the time, our family and three other families that rented some of the rooms. We had electricity, and even though it was curfew time, the light in the living room was on. Because of curfew we had installed a single red incandescent light in the living room to minimize reflection, enabling us to have some light during the curfew in effect from 6:00 p.m. until 7:00 a.m. Given the number of individuals under our roof, we needed some ability to talk quietly and visit with one another during the hours of curfew.

As soon as we heard the first sounds of gunfire, we immediately turned off the light and everyone ran to his or her room. I shared a room with my younger brother. We both lay on the floor under our bed. Lying in the darkness under my bed, I began to pray. I continually heard gunfire and each shot added new tension.

My body was shaking on the mat that separated me from the concrete underneath. I kept thinking about a Scripture that I had heard during the prayer meetings at St. Simon Baptist Church. The passage was Psalms 91:1–12, part of which states, ". . . he that dwells in the secret place of the most high shall abide under the shadow of the Almighty . . . ." I asked the lord in my prayers, "Lord, please deliver me from this war. If you deliver me, I will serve you for the rest of my life."

My family had lived in Monrovia for 19 years. On that night, at age 21, I prayed silently in the darkness of under my bed, fearing for my life and for those around me. Far from my mind were the pleasant memories of my exciting first glimpses of Monrovia. The interesting activity of the city with its large buildings, numerous lights, and many vehicles was replaced with darker images of buildings on fire and military vehicles on the roads. Civilians lay in darkness and silence while those armed took control. I prayed fervently beside my thirteen-year-old brother. At that time, neither of us understood or could have comprehended the severe reality of war. Thoughts and emotions were eclipsed by a prayerful desire to survive.

In that silence, I made a pledge to God that I would serve Him for the rest of my life if I could only survive. The prayer was sincere. I asked for peace and the opportunity to live beyond the violence to serve meaningfully. In humility, I confessed my prior resistance to fully yielding to God's will for my life. That night, shrouded by constant thought that my life could end at any moment, I realized the selfishness of my own plans and desired that they would be replaced with His purposes.

CHAPTER TWO

IMPRESSIONS FROM CHILDHOOD

I was born to the union of Mr. and Mrs. Samuel Dee Menyongar, Sr. Shortly after my birth in Boyah's Town, Rivercess County, Republic of Liberia, it was said that I would never be able to walk because my feet were dead. After many prayers and medical treatment by American missionaries from the Liberian Inland Mission, my feet gained strength and I started to walk at age two and a half. To God be the glory; nothing is impossible for God.

My mother's full name is Youborbah Dorothea Stewart. My parents hailed from Boyah's Town, the place of my birth. At the time of this writing, my mother is still alive and lives in Monrovia. She is presently 92 years old, an age not attained by many Liberians. My father, born in 1913, was reared by an Americo-Liberian, so he was brought up as Samuel Harris. He was a businessman and owned a dry cleaning shop. He was a founding member of the St. Simon Baptist Church in Bassa Community, Monrovia, Liberia. He served as a deacon for many years in this church until he went to be with the Lord on September 12, 1987.

Prior to my father's death, he experienced a number of medical challenges from 1984 through 1986. Those illnesses required him to go to the hospital periodically and to receive medical treatment. He knew that his days were limited. Early in 1987, he expressed his desire to live the final days of his life in the village where he was born. We honored his request. My mother, older sister, and some other relatives assisted in relocating and supporting him in the village in Boyah's Town, Rivercess County.

Due to the distance between Boyah's Town and Monrovia and my need to attend school, I was apart from my father during that time. I thought about him continually and prayed for him, asking the Lord for his protection and health. One thing I remember about my father is that he was a disciplinarian. He taught me to be content with that I had, to respect others, and to live up to my potential. He often stated that his desire was to see his children exceed the opportunities he had and the achievements that he made. He encouraged us to hold on to the Lord and to serve him. He modeled a steadfast life and looked out for what was best for his family.

When my father died in September 1987, he was laid to rest in the village burial place he had requested. He had wisely asked to move back to Boyah's Town to spend his final days in the land of his family. The location of his grave is very close to that of his older brother, his grandfather, and his great-grandfather. I am thankful to know that my father trusted God with his life.

In Africa we emphasize the importance of extended family, so my account would be incomplete if I did not mention my extended families. Our family is very large. My great-great-grandfather's name is Menyongar. My two great-grandfathers are Gboway and Boyah. Boyah had three sons and one daughter: Vonzea, Gboweah, Samuel Dee and Fannie. Gboweah had two children: Philip Weakon and Fanni. Vonzea had nine children: Philip, Jacob, Andrew, Thomas, Simeon, Enoch, Hannah, Ruth and Louis. Samuel has ten children already named above. Fanni had three children: Amos, Martha and Hannah. My grandfather from my mother's side is Gbar Stewart and my mother has brothers and sisters. Two of my uncles are Daniel and John. Most of my extended family live in villages and towns near the southeastern coast of Liberia.

I was born on April 19, 1966, as a fraternal twin. My twin sister, Magdalene, and I were born in Liberia's Inland Mission Hospital in Charlie's Town. I have four brothers and five sisters. My sisters are Martha, Julia, Sarah, Magdalene and Jannie. My brothers are Emmanuel, Edward (killed during the civil war in Liberia 1989-2003), Richard, and John.

My full name is David Samuel Gardayea Menyongar. David means *loving* or *to love*. Samuel means *heard of God*. Gardayea is a Bassa name. Bassa is one of the tribes in Liberia from the Kwa speaking group with the Kru, Grebo, Krahn, Sarpo and Deh, which means *man has come*. Menyongar means the *man who represents the weak ancestors*.

During our family meals when I was a child, we all used to eat together from one big bowl. Everyone ate with his or her hands. This method did not always work well. Most of my brothers ate very fast, leaving little food for me. Tired of the situation, I slapped the hands and faces of those who ate quickly. This led to fighting. Sometimes, in utter frustration, I threw the bowl on the ground. After a few instances, my mother beat me mercilessly and peppered me in the eyes, nose and ears. My punishment was so great, I quit fighting for food.

When we lived in Boyah's Town and were not attending school (I was too young at that time anyway), we helped our parents to go on the farm and help to plant rice or drive birds from coming to eat the seeds. We also helped our parents set traps for animals that came on the farm such as deer, rabbits, and squirrels. It was on the farm that our mother and older sisters would cook and we would have our lunch. They cooked and we ate in a barn-like structure made of corner poles and a roof made of palm thatch and grasses used for roofing materials. Those days were hot, usually around 90+ degrees Fahrenheit and we enjoyed the cooler shaded area.

When the sun went down, we would leave the farm area and go back to the village. Usually our father was in front and our mother at the back with our sisters. The little children walked near our father, who carried a cutlass or hoe in his hand. We also tried to help by carrying other items such as rope, knives, cups, and plates.

In our village after the evening meal, we often made a big fire and sat around it. While our sisters played, we boys sat with our father around the fire. He told us stories about spiders, monkeys, and how our great-grand-fathers fought to get the land we were living on and that we should follow their footsteps. Sometimes our father told us how he went to Monrovia during the Second World War and how he worked for the American soldiers that were assigned at Roberts International Airport. He stayed with some of them and they gave him the name Samuel Harris. He mentioned how they wanted to take him to the USA but his older brother told him not to go.

I remember Christmas and New Year's Day as times for great celebration. We ate so much food and men came to our village to play music. There was also a church in our village since one of our uncles was a pastor with the Open Bible Standard missions. My uncle was a very prayerful man. Rev. Vonyea Menyongar and many missionaries visited our village because of the work that he did.

We also used to travel with our father to attend church conferences around Rivercess. At times, we walked for two or three days to get to the conference if no vehicle was available. Usually, a vehicle was only available on main roads and then only about once a week. My father

32

attended those conferences as part of his role as a deacon. He went as a representative of our church and sometimes he would take me or one of my brothers and sisters along. Usually, my mother did not attend due to her home responsibilities.

Our father set firm expectations for the children. He would discipline us by using a cane from a bamboo plant to strike us. Those strikes were applied to our back or buttocks or hands. The punishment was painful but effective in correcting behavior. My mother typically used a different approach, as did most of the other women in that area. When we misbehaved as children she would usually put pepper in our eyes and nose to teach us a lesson. That method, too, was painful but convincing. Overall, my siblings and I were well behaved because we knew what our parents expected.

Early in my life, my Christian parents taught me how to pray and to go to church. My father was a deacon in the Baptist Church and my mother was a leader in the Inland Mission Church, an American church with a strong missionary focus. Since my father was a deacon, it was mandatory for all of us to go to church. Our parents brought us all up in the fear of the Lord. As we grew up, we went to church every Sunday morning and evening and to the midweek service on Wednesday evening and prayer meeting on Friday.

I enjoyed my Sunday School class and Children's Church. We were taught many stories from the Bible and learned memory verses. Some of my favorites were David and Goliath, Moses and Pharaoh, Daniel in the lions' den, Joseph and his brothers, and Shadrach, Meshach and Abednego in the fiery furnace. I memorized verses also, including John 3:16, John 11:35, John 1:12, John 14:1 and 6, and Romans 3:23 and 6:23.

No one was to work on Sunday; that day was observed as day of rest. I remembered we wanted to play football so we decided to wash our clothes on Sunday but our father refused to allow us to do the laundry and did not permit us to go play soccer on Sunday. We could not pound cassava or cassava leaves on Sunday even if this was the food we were to eat. I recall later that I was not permitted to repair a door or wooden window on Sunday.

I used to help my father by going to the church with him and sweeping. When the adults prayed, my brothers, sisters, and I joined with my father to pray. Usually my father and other deacons would kneel down and pray and sing some songs from the Baptist hymnal. They sang songs like "I Surrender All," "Just As I Am," and "More about Jesus." Sometimes they conducted fasting and prayer at the church. I played an active part in the Sunday School Department, Youth Department, Youth Choir, Royal Ambassadors and the Boy Scouts.

In 1971, our family moved to Monrovia, Liberia's capital city. We moved into our father's house in Bassa Community. In Monrovia, living with our parents was different from Boyah Town, Rivercess. In Monrovia we lived in a house of eleven rooms with ten children, our father and mother, and with uncles and aunties and cousins. In addition, three families rented rooms in our father's house from Maryland, Grand Gedeh, and Nimba counties. All of those counties played principal parts in the war that engulfed Liberia later.

Life was much different in Monrovia. In our village we used to walk about two miles to the river to fetch water and then we climbed a hill, carrying the water we needed. We got water at the river to drink, to cook, to wash our dishes, to take a bath, and it was in this same river that we did our laundry. In Monrovia, there were cars, soft drinks, electricity and running water.

One night, when I was five years old, I fell from my bed. My body dropped onto a lantern that cut my face badly. I was rushed to the hospital where I had stitches and stayed for two weeks of treatment. I still bear the scar on my forehead today. God also saw me through that accident because the laceration was very deep and the injury could have affected me for the rest of my life.

In Monrovia, we had to fetch water from the public pump early in the morning, clean the house, and prepare for school. We walked to school and our school was not far from where we lived. We came back from school in the afternoon and helped our mother to cook. Saturday was a time to do laundry and to clean. On Saturday, we usually ate Fufu or Dumboy, which is a staple food for the Bassa tribal group in Liberia. Fufu or Dumboy is made from cassava roots. On Sunday we went to church.

We were introduced to the Monrovian life quickly by our friends and relatives. Most of our friends in Monrovia could speak English. My brothers and sisters and I could not until 1971 when my parents moved to Monrovia, the capital city of Liberia. Other children our age provoked us and threatened us not to use the main road until we learned to speak English.

During my growing up years, if anyone attacked a member of my family, they had to face all of the rest of us. One day we were going to school when a group of boys stopped us and told us to go back home. They claimed that we came from the village and knew nothing. We refused and they insisted that we could not pass to go to school. We went back home to tell our father and he told us to go to school. My father said, "If you do not go to school, then I will punish you."

At that time, my siblings and I decided to fight back. This decision was a turning point for us. We mixed English with the local Bassa dialect and warned them, "The next time we are attacked, we will destroy all of you!" Their reaction initially was one of fear and surprise because they saw our determination and sensed that we were willing to fight to the end. Later we had to back up our warning. We used all the fighting techniques that we had learned in the village, like going under a person and attacking them. In the city the boys knew how to fight like Bruce Lee or Mohammed Ali. We used a more scrappy, villager approach! After knocking two or three of them down, they ran and left us. This unity in our family caused people to be afraid to mistreat us. Later, those who bullied us became our friends instead of enemies.

My childhood was very difficult. What my friends could do easily, I struggled to accomplish. For example, playing soccer or running for me was very difficult. One day we had a running race in front of our home and my friends defeated me every time. Each time my father told me that I should make it or should not get tired or give up. My father especially motivated me to keep trying in most of the things I did, whether it was in education or physical pursuits such as soccer or running. He insisted that I could achieve what others did if I would just be determined.

One morning in 1973, I was sitting on an old wooden chair near a coal pot where our mother boiled water for bathing before we went to school. My chair turned over and I fell into the scorching water. My back and legs were badly burned. I was taken to the hospital and treated by Dr. Whitsiner. I was hospitalized for three months for second-degree burns. Thankfully, the Lord healed me, but the scars are still on my body. Determination was my watch word in everything I did. To this day, these words of assurance have helped me tremendously.

Even though I grew up in a Christian home, I did not have a personal relationship with the Lord Jesus Christ. Nevertheless, I was faithful in attending church. In 1980, while in Junior High School (seventh grade), I joined the Lawana Christian Fellowship, a branch of the Scripture Union of Liberia. I attended camps and retreats and later became a member of the Teen Time Quiz Team of the Bassa Teenage Junior High School.

We were trained in Bible memorization and recitation. We practiced regularly after school and held inter-junior high quiz competitions. These were held at the Monrovia City Hall with thousands in attendance. The program was aired over the radio. There was a quizmaster and a panel who asked questions. Quiz team participants competed to be the first to jump to their feet and answer the questions.

During this period, a missionary visited on a short-term mission trip to Liberia with the Youth of Christ. Her name was Sister Jessica, and she led me to the Lord Jesus Christ. She told me, "Going to church does not make a person saved. To be saved you must confess with your mouth the Lord Jesus Christ and believe in your heart that God raised him from the grave. Then you are saved." She cited Romans 10:9–10 and Ephesians 2:8, which states that it is by grace that you are saved and it is not by work, neither any man should boast. I do not know where Sister Jessica is, but if she ever reads this book, I would like to see her and thank her for leading me to the Lord. I am also praying for her that God will continue to bless her.

After I was born again (got saved), I told my parents and they were happy and went to church the next Sunday and told our pastor. The pastor brought me before the church and introduced me to the congregation. He said, "Since you were not ashamed of the Lord Jesus Christ before men, he will not be ashamed of you before his Father."

My salvation gave me peace and a strong hope. I am fortunate that our country was not divided by war's violence during my formative years. When I grew up in Monrovia, our country was at peace. Armed soldiers did not occupy the streets; they were confined to the military barracks. Looking back at my childhood memories enables me to see a tranquil time period in Liberian history. Pleasant memories from that pre-war era were nearly pushed beyond my reach by the partitions of violence. Thanks to God, those memories were not completely overtaken.

CHAPTER THREE

ESCAPE TO
BUSHROD ISLAND

At some point I must have fallen asleep after I prayed under my bed and asked God to save me. I awoke at about 5:00 a.m. on July 9, 1990, lying under my bed on the floor. There had been little rest for me, the first of many sleepless nights that lay ahead. I had prayed myself to sleep, asking the Lord to deliver my family, friends, and me. Thoughts and images of people I knew swirled in my mind as I prayed for them, suddenly realizing that how war affects everything and everybody. Finally, I had drifted off to sleep, tiredness giving way to the sounds of combat that filled the air. When I first woke up I saw my brother lying near me under the bed.

"Pekin John, wake up, wake up," I whispered quietly. (My brother's name was John, but we called him Pekin John because Pekin is a name used for a little one or a younger brother.)

He opened his eyes and yawned widely cradling his head in his hands.

"We must get prepared to leave now," I told him.

"Where will we go?" he asked.

"We'll go to Bushrod Island," I replied.

"It will be safer there and my friend Emmanuel Paulus has an auntie there with a place we can stay. It's near the Iron Factory community." (Emmanuel's father was a deacon in a Baptist Church where my father also had served as a deacon before he died in 1987. Emmanuel's father had always been an encouragement to our family, and he had often told me that he knew God would use my life.)

"How do I know that the place is safe?" Pekin John asked, a little more alertly.

I explained, "This fellow called Prince Johnson, the leader of the Independent National Patriotic Front is in charge of the island. I heard that he is giving food to people. If anyone is caught stealing from anyone, that person will be executed immediately."

At the time, my main concerns were security and food. I had heard about Bushrod Island from people going there before the attack on Monrovia. Since the first rumors and news of war spread across Monrovia, people had sought food. I knew some people from our community who had been to Bushrod Island to get food and had come back. Others went and did not come back because they felt safe there and knew that things were uncertain in Monrovia. My friend Emmanuel had moved to Bushrod Island to live with his auntie. I had not spoken with Emmanuel since he left for the island, but I had been to the island in 1989 to attend a youth service at Grace Baptist Church. I knew how to get to Bushrod Island, which was about fifteen miles away, and I thought I could find Emmanuel.

"If you think that's where we'll be safe, then we should go," answered Pekin John.

Although we normally bathed after waking, we only brushed our teeth that morning. Then we each got a plastic bag and put in an extra pair of trousers and a shirt, a toothbrush, and a comb. I also grabbed a notebook and a pen, and we prepared to exit our room and leave for Bushrod Island.

From the table in our room, I picked up my student identification card from the University of Liberia. I had seen enough news reports featuring images of beheaded members of the Gio and Mano tribes to know that proper identification could mean the difference between life and death. I placed my identification card in my pocket—a safer place than the plastic bag—and thought about Pekin John.

"Pekin John, do you have your ID card with you also?"

He looked in his book bag, the one he carried with him each day to Monrovia Demonstration School, and pulled out his sixth-grade ID card. "Yes, I have it," he replied and put it in his pocket.

In the house, the others were packing quickly and quietly. Light from dawn streamed through the cracks in the wooden windows. The near silence was in contrast to the sounds of gunfire that had filled the air just a few hours earlier. Now the only sounds were the result of nervous individuals moving about in preparation to leave the city. Occasionally, I could hear neighbors outside their houses trying to leave as quietly as possible.

Neither of my parents was in our house at the time of the attack. My father had passed away in 1987. My mother had traveled upcountry along with Edward, my thirty-three-year-old brother months previously. Emmanuel, my thirty-six-year-old brother was away teaching in Grand Bassa County near Rivercess, the village where I was born. Members of my immediate family who were in our house at the time of the attack included Sarah, my twenty-nine-year-old sister; Magdalene, my twin sister (we were twenty-four at that time); Richard, my twenty-three-year-old brother; Jannie, my twenty-two-year-old sister; and Pekin John, my thirteen-year-old brother. Others in the house during the attack included two aunties, one uncle, two cousins, four nephews, two nieces, and two other families who rented rooms. Also there was a classmate of mine from junior high school who had recently come to stay with us. His name was Joshua Vaye, and he was from the Gio tribe. He had come to stay with us because the Gio tribe members were hunted by the faction of the AFL that was loyal to Samuel Doe.

When Pekin John and I emerged from our room to leave for Bushrod Island, my sister Sarah asked, "Where are you going?"

"To Bushrod Island," I replied, "I don't think the Bassa Community is safe any longer."

"We're going to Rivercess where our mother is. I think it will be safer for me and the children." She planned to take two nephews and one niece with her.

"If you think that is safe for you, then fine. I don't believe it will be safe because it's the direction that Charles Taylor's men are coming from," I answered.

"The rebels have already passed there, and they did not destroy it," she said. "We'll go there."

The conversation with my sister was short and occurred as we prepared to leave. All of us were afraid to talk in a normal tone of voice, so we kept our voices low. I remember having a similar exchange with my sister Jannie.

"I'm planning to stay here," stated Jannie. "It's probably the safest for me."

"They will come back and attack," I responded.

"I don't think this fighting will last long," Jannie replied confidently. "I'll stay."

Magdalene decided to go in the same direction as Sarah, heading to River Cess.

Along with Jannie, Richard decided to stay. The extended family members also decided to stay. Joshua decided to go to St. Peter Lutheran Church in the Sinkor area of Monrovia.

All of the planning and discussion of plans occurred quickly. By 7:30 a.m. each of us had decided where to go and briefly said goodbye. The abruptness of the farewells made them not seem real. War had brought about separation and forced decisions that would not normally be taken. There was no time to waste.

My brother and I walked out of our house and began our journey to Bushrod Island. We had not walked far before I saw dead bodies on the side of the road. Smoke rose from buildings and houses that had been burned. Military trucks and vehicles dominated the roads; no other private or commercial vehicles dared use the roads. Those who did try to drive their own vehicles were often killed by the military and the vehicles were commandeered for military use.

During this period of time there was total confusion. Thousands of civilians walked in many different directions, hoping to find safety and food. Some fled toward Bushrod Island; others entered Monrovia in hopes that the city would be safest; others left Monrovia in all directions. The chaos was partly controlled by strategic military checkpoints. Some members of the AFL loyal to Samuel Doe had set up military check- points where everyone was asked for identification. Those manning the checkpoints were looking for members of the Gio and Mano tribes and any other person who could not provide proper identification. Members of the Gio or Mano tribes and those without proper identification were killed immediately.

After walking for about thirty minutes, Pekin John and I crossed Gabriel Tucker Bridge and entered Vai Town, an area on the southern tip of Bushrod Island. Vai Town and the community near it, Samuel Doe Community, were controlled by the AFL members loyal to Doe. Prince Johnson and the INPFL controlled most of Bushrod Island, including the Port of Monrovia. As a result, the area including Gabriel Tucker Bridge, Vai Town, and Samuel Doe Community formed a battle line between the area occupied by the INPFL and the AFL members loyal to Doe. Shortly after crossing the bridge that led to Bushrod Island, we faced our first military checkpoint. Getting through that checkpoint meant that we could enter the area of Bushrod Island controlled by Prince Johnson and the INPFL, the area that we felt would be safest.

A long line had formed on the sidewalk leading to the checkpoint where armed soldiers asked for identification and determined whether

40

or not to allow passage further into Bushrod Island. Surrounding those asking for identification were scores of heavily armed soldiers. Spiked sticks had been placed across the road to stop all but military vehicles from passing through. Peking John and I found our place in line.

Most of those in line were men. From the beginning of the conflict women and girls were afraid to be in public. Women and girls feared that they would be taken by soldiers or rebels and raped or taken as slaves or both. Around Pekin John and me in line were mainly young men trying to get to Bushrod Island. We also saw men with their wives and children. Some of the women carried on their heads some of their family's most needed or most valuable possessions wrapped in lappas. (A lappa is a common name for cloth that women often tie around them to carry children or loose items.) The stuffed lappas of various mixed colors—green, red, blue, yellow and others—indicated that many were fleeing Monrovia with no intention to return soon.

Armed rebel at checkpoint

We stood in line for nearly an hour listening to the raised voices of the armed soldiers harshly questioning those who reached the checkpoint. By watching the treatment of those men who were denied passage through the checkpoint, we knew that we were between life and death. I did not talk to Pekin John, but I prayed silently that God would spare us. I was not highly concerned about Pekin John being able to get through the checkpoint. I was concerned about having to present an identification card from the University of Liberia.

41

I knew that I might not get any sympathy after the soldiers knew that I was student of the University of Liberia. About three years previous, in 1987, many students at the University of Liberia had organized protests against the government led by Samuel Doe. In the wake of those protests, there had been clashes between members of the AFL loyal to Doe and students at the university. Several students had been arrested; some were killed.

The friction between Doe's army and students of the University of the Liberia was on my mind. Just two weeks prior to the attack on the Bassa Community on July 8, 1990, the leader of the student union at the University of Liberia had been killed. The student leader, Woi Tapei, was killed in Jallah Town near the Bassa Community. Tapei, a member of the Mano tribe, was murdered as he tried to leave the country. Tapei's death was most likely caused merely by a grudge resulting from the clashes between students and the AFL. I knew that he had done nothing to deserve death because I served alongside him as a member of the Student Unification Party that helped Tapei get elected to lead the student government. In addition to the grudge, there was also probably fear that Tapei might join the rebels and use his leadership skills to strengthen their forces.

As I stood in line beside Pekin John, I thought about Tapei, and in my heart I prayed that I would not be victimized. I prayed, "Lord, create an opportunity that will enable us to pass." Unlike Tapei, I was not a member of the Mano tribe, and I thought that might work in my favor.

As the sun crept higher and we felt the July heat typical in Liberia, Pekin John and I inched closer to the checkpoint. With each step I grew more tense. I glanced at Pekin John quickly out of the corner of my eye. I intentionally did not make eye contact with him as we approached the checkpoint. We did not want to raise the suspicion of those checking IDs. Several soldiers armed with AK-47s stood before us. We stepped forward unsure of which soldier would check our identification. I continued to pray silently that God would allow us to pass the checkpoint. I could tell by the shape of their faces and their accents that the soldiers checking IDs were members of the Krahn tribe. As we stepped forward the soldier that acknowledged us was an older man. He asked, "Where are you coming from?"

I replied, "From the Bassa Community with my younger brother."

He looked at Pekin John and asked him, "Is it true that he is your brother?"

"Yes, he is my older brother," Pekin John answered.

"What is his name?" the soldier asked, wanting to verify that we really were brothers.

Pekin John answered, "David S. Menyongar." (In Liberia, people called me by my first name. My father's name was Samuel, so I was called David to distinguish between us.)

Turning to me, the soldier said, "Let me see your ID."

I pulled my ID from my pocket and handed it to him. I noticed that when I handed it to him that the ID was upside down. At that moment I knew that the soldier could not read. He stared at the ID for several moments and then asked, "Which unit do you belong to."

His question confused me and I didn't know how to answer. I dared not laugh or ask what he meant for fear that he would suspect that I knew he could not read. I did not want to embarrass him. I replied with the first answer that I thought of. "Unit A," I replied.

With a gesture that brought relief, the soldier returned my University of Liberia identification card to me. As his AK-47 moved with the motion of his arm moving forward, he said, "You people can go." He never asked for Pekin John's ID. Immediately, I knew that God had answered my prayers. At that time, I knew God's presence was with us. I was joyful in my heart but could not say anything until long after we passed through the checkpoint on our way deeper into Bushrod Island.

After passing through the checkpoint, we walked along the road called Freeway that led toward New Georgia Estates, a low-cost housing area on Bushrod Island. We walked in that direction to find Emmanuel at his auntie's house. When we were safely away from the checkpoint, I turned to Pekin John. I said, "I am sure it was God who intervened to keep me from being arrested by the soldier at the checkpoint because university students are enemies to them." I went on to tell Pekin John about my friend who had been killed by the AFL soldiers loyal to Doe.

Pekin John replied, "It's true that it was God who did it."

Knowing that there was not much threat around us, I asked if he noticed how the soldier at the checkpoint had turned my ID upside down. Pekin John had not noticed the soldier turn my card upside down, but we laughed together about it. After we laughed about the incident, I said, "It's true that most people who join the army are not educated." He agreed with me, and we continued our walk still smiling about the incident and thankful that God had allowed us to pass through.

As we walked along the road, we felt much safer than we had in Bassa Community, and we were glad that we decided to flee from Monrovia to Bushrod Island. On the island, the civilians moved about with little concern for their safety. The INPFL provided protection, and in Freeport there were also food distribution areas. The INPFL wanted to be in good relationship with the civilians because Prince Johnson, Charles Taylor, and Samuel Doe were competing for control of the country. Charles Taylor and the NPFL already controlled much of the country. Samuel Doe controlled mainly the area around Monrovia, and support for Doe was very low. Although Prince Johnson controlled only Bushrod Island, he held a strategic advantage by controlling the Port of Monrovia—known as Freeport. As a result, the INPFL had access to supplies of food, vehicles, petroleum, and the main point of entrance to and exit from Liberia. (The airports were closed due to war.)

Civilians on Bushrod Island enjoyed the presence of the INPFL and benefits they provided in order to stay in good relations with the people. In fact, Bushrod Island was one of the few areas that had access to electricity at that time. INPFL soldiers were easily recognized by their full military fatigues and their signature red scarves tied around their necks. INPFL vehicles moved quickly up and down the road transporting troops and supplies to various points on the island where conflict was expected. The daily lives of most civilians were disrupted due to war, even though the conflict had not yet spread to Bushrod Island. In addition to the INPFL forces preparing for war, the civilians either headed to Freeport or they remained where they lived and prepared for war. As we walked, we saw many people selling "gold dust" (rice) and other food items that were in high demand. Rice was called "gold dust" during the war because it was in such high demand.

By late afternoon, we arrived at the community called Iron Factory, a community named after all the many pieces of scrap metal that were found throughout the area. This was the community where Emmanuel lived with his auntie. Her house was near a swamp on the east side of Bushrod Island across from Freeport. When Pekin John and I walked up the house, Emmanuel and his brother Timothy ran out to greet us. They were glad to see us because they had heard that there had been fighting in the Bassa Community. I was surprised to see so many people. Many others had fled to the house from Monrovia and other parts of the country. There were many acquaintances with the family through church involvement and relatives. About 50 people were staying at Emmanuel's auntie's house even though it only had two bedrooms. Most slept on the floor, which was normal during war. Even the older people who slept on mattresses placed them on the floor to stay as low as possible for safety.

We stayed at Emmanuel's auntie's house for about a week. On the evening of our arrival, the large group of people staying there gathered for prayer. We prayed for protection for family and friends and for the war to come to an end. We prayed for protection for each other. After a time of prayer, we moved around the crowded house to find a place to sleep. In the distance, we heard the sound of heavy combat from the Monrovia area. The fighting sounded much more intense than it had been the night before when we fell under attack. Looking out of the windows, we saw buildings on fire, huge red flames rising against the dark sky over Monrovia. Occasional blasts sounded like bomb explosions. In the darkness of the crowded house, we lay down and prayed silently, concerned about friends and family members.

Each morning and evening during our stay at the Iron Factory community, we gathered for prayer. Every night, we could hear fighting from the Monrovia area. We knew the soldiers were resting during the day and fighting by night. Food was scarce; we mainly ate potato leaves with salt and pepper or fruit from palm trees. Every morning when we woke up some of the younger ones usually fainted because of hunger. We could not even use the outdoor latrine as normal because there was not even food in our stomachs. All of the 50 or so people taking refuge at Emmanuel's auntie's house were concerned about their friends and family and wondered often whether they would see them again.

After we had been at Emmanuel's auntie's house about a week, someone reported suspicious movement of people in uniform in the nearby swamp area. The INPFL suspected that AFL soldiers were trying to enter the area through the swamp. That night in addition to the sounds of combat in the distance toward Monrovia, there were also sounds of gunfire close by. We could hear bullets whizzing through the air throughout the night. From the direction of the sounds, it seemed that the INPFL outnumbered those trying to move through the swamp.

Even before the fighting broke out in the area surrounding the Iron Factory community, Emmanuel, his brother, Pekin John, and I had been discussing leaving due to lack of food. Pekin John continued to ask to leave, stating that he could not bear the hunger. I noticed how he had changed and knew that because other children were fainting each day, the health concerns were real. As a result of hunger as well as the presence of fighting nearby and getting closer, the four of us decided to leave.

Emmanuel told his auntie that the four of us were leaving to look for food. She agreed to let us go only because of the extreme circumstances. The chances of us safely finding food were not good. Out of concern for us, she warned us multiple times about keeping safe. We understood her anxiety; we too were uncertain about what lay ahead. Her cautions and our own doubts filled our thoughts as we prepared to venture into the unknown.

CHAPTER FOUR

HISTORY LESSONS

As a child I attended the Pilgrim Foundation Elementary School located in the Bassa Community in Monrovia. I enjoyed attending school and found great satisfaction in learning. In particular, I liked learning about the history of Liberia as well as the region of West Africa.

Studying Liberia's history filled me with a sense of pride about my native country. After the war, that sense of pride became entwined with a sense of sorrow regarding the tragic events. The history narrative of Liberia is no less important to me now. Woven into that story, however, are the elements that led to Liberia's brutal Civil War.

Liberia was established through the efforts of the American Colonization Society, whose members advocated for the repatriation of Black Americans to Africa ("The Lone Star," 2002). The first group of freed slaves, later referred to as Americo-Liberians, were settled on Providence Island in 1822. The name Liberia stems from the Latin word *liber*, which means "free" ("Liberia," 2014). To validate the name, a motto was chosen: "The love of liberty brought us here." The capital city (initially named Christopolis, meaning "the City of Christ") was later named after U.S. President James Monroe in 1824 ("The Lone Star," 2002).

On July 26, 1847, Liberia declared independence as a republic ("Liberia Gains Independence," 2013). It is one of the nations in Africa that was not colonized by any world empire. The ex-slaves that led Liberia copied what they had seen during their years of slavery in America. For example, the flag of Liberia is similar to that of the United States of America, except it has one white star on a blue square and 11 horizontal stripes alternating red and white. The constitution is also similar, and from 1847 to 1985 the currency used in Liberia was the U.S. dollar.

Liberia was founded on Christian principles. Enshrined in the constitution is the fundamental declaration that Liberia is a Christian nation and that there will always be freedom of religion. The Americo-Liberians, or freed slaves, ruled or led the government of Liberia until 1980, a period of 133 years.

Among African nations, Liberia has traditionally had a fairly strong economy. Before the Civil War, it was regarded as one of the most stable and peaceful countries in West Africa. Many nationals from other African countries went there to work and save money that they then spent in their native developing countries. Liberia boasted one of the world's largest rubber plantations. It also produced the second female President of the UN General Assembly: the Honorable Angie Elisabeth Brooks-Randolph ("Angie Elisabeth Brooks-Randolph," n.d.). Liberia was a founding member of the UN, the Organisation of African Unity, which is now the African Union (AU), and the Economic Community of West African States (ECOWAS).

When I was in the sixth grade at the Lorma Community School, an event occurred that I will never forget. On April 12, 1980, a sergeant of the Armed Forces of Liberia (AFL), Samuel Kanyon Doe, from Grand Gedeh County in the eastern part of Liberia, overthrew the True Whig Party led government of William R. Tolbert. In that coup, Tolbert was killed. Thirteen of Tolbert's cabinet ministers were tried by a special tribunal set up by the PRC. The tribunal found all 13 guilty.

The trials of Tolbert's cabinet ministers were held in various government buildings in Monrovia, not too far from where my family lived. The men were sentenced to death. On the day of the execution, the men sentenced were stripped to their underwear. They were led handcuffed through the streets of Monrovia as soldiers forced them to march to the Barclay's Training Center, a military barracks near the beach.

Great crowds gathered to watch the march and the execution. Some of my siblings and young friends followed the convicted cabinet ministers among the thousands of onlookers. I watched as the men to be executed were lined against 13 poles on the beach. Soldiers removed their handcuffs and tied their wrists to the poles behind them their backs. Soldiers then placed large white rice bags over the heads of each of the convicted men. In their final minutes, the men stood on the beach, their backs to the water and their covered heads facing the crowds. I remember seeing the waters of the Atlantic behind the men, ready to receive the bullets that would pass through them on that sunny day.

That scene influenced my view of politics. At the young age of 14, I associated politics with danger. I realized that a person could work hard for many years trying to achieve change for a better society only to lose all that he had fought and sacrificed for due to a takeover of leadership. Since that time, my view of politics has been negatively influenced. Even now when I think about politics, my mind is drawn to that day on the beach when I and thousands of my fellow Liberians heard the commander order the execution.

Time slowed as the soldiers facing the convicted men raised their automatic weapons. In the ensuing moments, round after round of shots were fired at each body. Smoke rose as dead bodies slumped. The commander ordered, "Cease fire," only after enough rounds had been fired to convince those watching that no life remained in the bodies of the convicted men. Many in the crowd shed tears, but all restrained their emotions, knowing that an open expression would indicate support of the overthrown government.

As a result of the coup d'état, my school and other schools across the country shut down for a long period of time. Eventually, the schools reopened after a period of calm had been established. Sgt. Samuel Doe established a military junta called The People's Redemption Council (PRC) and selected young officers like himself to be part of this council. In the initial stages, the PRC did extremely well. Since they were inexperienced soldiers-politicians, they brought on board politicians from different political parties. For the next several years, Liberia experienced a period of peace and prosperity.

In November of 1985, I was a senior in high school. I had gained a year due to my transition from Booker T. Washington Institute to R.C. Lawson Institute. When they evaluated my academics, I received a double promotion, effectively advancing a grade. As a senior in high school I studied to sit for my national exams called the West Africa National Exams. During that time, I witnessed one of the first democratic elections in Liberia. The head of the military junta, Samuel K. Doe, won the elections conducted by Emma Harmon, Chairman of the National Election Commission. Other parties cried foul and said that the elections were rigged by Samuel Doe. As a result, there were numerous demonstrations to protest the elections results. During this time Liberia started to experience instability and there were glimpses of chaos, but no one thought that we would enter into a civil war. This was the beginning of terrible things unfolding.

The tension kept mounting until the night of December 24, 1989, when the National Patriotic Front of Liberia (NPFL) attacked Liberia from Burtuo, Nimba County. That violence hindered my education and the education of tens of thousands of other children as war emerged. At that point, my school-based study of history stopped along with the shut-down of Liberia's educational system. Little did any of us know that we were on the front edge of a war that would last for 14 years. I had enjoyed studying history in school; however, when studying past wars, I did not think that I would experience war in my lifetime.

One of the interesting aspects about the history of Liberia is the influence of the many ethnic groups within the country. The minority Americo-Liberians (approximately 5% of the population) have ruled Liberia for most of its history. As I learned in my history and social studies classes, three major tribal groups are represented, and each of those include further subsets. One of those major ethnic groups is the Mande, which also includes Belle, Gissi, Gola, Kpelle, Mandingo, Mende, and Vai. Another is the Kwa, which includes Bassa, Dey, Gibi, Grebo, Krahn, Kru, and Sarpo. A third major ethnic group is the Mel, which includes the following: Dahn, Gio, Mano, and Lorma.

The presence of so many ethnic groups has resulted in conflicts throughout the history of Liberia. Reasons for the fighting are similar to the source of conflicts in other nations: disputes over land, efforts to establish ethnic supremacy, and competition for government leadership. Father Robert Tikpor, regarded as the national orator of Liberia, delivered a speech in July 2010 about the need for national unity. In that speech, he commented on the history of intertribal conflicts in Liberia as summarized in the excerpt below.

> "In our own country, before the settlers came to found
> Liberia, there were frequent intertribal wars; especially,
> during the two hundred years (1619 – 1816) when
> slaves were captured, collected, from among the tribes
> fighting each other. Before slavery began, these inter-
> tribal wars were fought over land, wealth, and other
> matters that were offensive to one or the other tribe.
> For example, there was a war between the Bassas and
> Kpelles. How do we know about these wars? From
> maxims often repeated by the Bassas like

'Glewetae Dju Dje a Kpah Kpeletoh', and again 'Zainkpa da mehn Kpeleh da Coatin Kpo.'

We wouldn't have known about these wars but for the maxims that have come down to us. In the first maxim, the Bassas are saying that Glewetae was a little man who was so small in body that the children saw and thought that he was one of them. So they invited him to join them and go against the Kpelle, but he displayed such warlike deeds that his deeds were cited for generations yet unborn to emulate. His heroic feats became themes for a ballad to him since then.

In the second maxim, 'Zainkpa is dead and so the Kpelle man has worn a coat,' Zainkpa was a Kpelle man who was captured by the Bassa warriors and he was disowned by his own kinsmen. But the Bassas honored him as brave a captive. Therefore they kept him. But in order to retaliate against his own people, Zainkpa swore to his ancestral spirits that any Kpelle man who ever crossed his path would be captured and sold into slavery. From Zainkpa's death, this ballad was sung and began to spread far and wide among the Bassa people." ("National July 26 Oration," 2010)

The historical information provided by Father Tikpor illustrates the long tension of intertribal conflicts and rivalries among different groups in Liberia. Those ancient conflicts created divisions that were partly the foundation for strife in modern times. As referenced in the next excerpt from Father Tikpor's same speech, even the idea that fighters in the Liberian Civil War could have special powers is rooted in the country's historical narrative. Father Tikpor stated:

"These intertribal wars were not only between tribes. When the Settlers came, there were wars between them and some ethnic groups. For instance, a battle was fought between the combined forces of the Dey, Vai, and Mamban Bassa ethnic groups and the settlers at Fort Hill on December 1, 1822. In that battle, Matilda Newport is alleged to have been the heroine, and until recently did her alleged exploits come to be questioned by some Liberian historians. Mind you, those native warriors were imbued with the mystic idea that no bullet or cannon fire could put them to flight when they had taken a magic portion in their blood. This conviction informed modern perspectives as we heard amongst most of the fighters who partook in our Civil War. Doe is said to have sent some of his fighters to the practitioners of this 'bullet proof' magic. ("National July 26 Oration," 2010)

Due to those historical ethnic conflicts, there existed enmity between some of the tribes of Liberia. When the war started in 1989 it revived the old wounds. People took sides based on ethnic allegiance. Although Charles Taylor was an Americo-Liberian, he was knowledgeable about the historical intertribal conflicts. Part of his strategy must have been the age-old maxim "Divide and conquer."

In reviewing the accounts of the war, it seems obvious that Taylor leveraged intertribal division to his advantage. For example, Taylor enlisted rebel troops within his National Patriotic Front of Liberia (NPFL) who were mainly of the Gio/Mano tribes. That point is important because Quiwonkpa, the person accused of attempting to overthrow President Doe in 1985, was a Gio. He had been well respected among the Gio and Mano tribes. Doe had him killed in 1985, which created the basis for a grudge.

The Gio/Mano grudge was targeted toward the Krahn/Sarpo tribes. President Doe was of the Krahn ethnicity. Over time, he favored Krahns to the point that his national army, the Armed Forces of Liberia (AFL), predominantly was composed of Krahn/Sarpo soldiers. Ethnicity emerged as a major catalyst for killings early in the Civil War. Gio/Mano rebels sought revenge on Krahn/Sarpo forces, most of which were loyal to Doe.

One of Taylor's NPFL commanders, Prince Y. Johnson, a Mano from Nimba County, formed the Independent National Patriotic Front of Liberia (INPFL) in 1990. That small faction proved disproportionately strong under the skillful leadership of Prince Johnson, who had been trained in the U.S. in military tactics. After breaking away from the NPFL, Prince Johnson successfully led his much smaller group in overtaking about half of the capital city of Monrovia. This occurred because Prince Johnson and his troops moved faster than the larger NPFL.

In September 1990, Prince Johnson and his troops captured Doe in a surprising manner. Doe had been invited to meet with the commander of ECOMOG (Economic Community of West African States Monitoring Group) to negotiate a governmental transition. The goal of ECOMOG was to convince Doe to step down as President, leave the country, and live in immunity in Nigeria. That transition was viewed as a means to prevent the conflict from spreading. Doe had resisted such attempts at negotiation on multiple occasions prior to September 1990.

For the first time, Doe agreed to meet in a port area near Monrovia called Freeport, the location of the ECOMOG headquarters. Prior to the meeting, an unknown informant tipped off Prince Johnson with details about the arrangement. Doe and his Executive Mansion Guards arrived in Freeport for the meeting with the ECOMOG commander, General Arnold Quinoo. Doe's guards were directed to put down their weapons as they entered the headquarters of the peacekeeping force.

While Doe met with General Quinoo, Prince Johnson and his men secretly prepared for their quick strike. At the right time, Prince Johnson and his men stormed the ECOMOG headquarters with such haste and firepower that they easily broke through the ECOMOG guards.

The ECOMOG guards were part of a peacekeeping mission, so they were not expecting a fight in that neutral zone. Quickly, Prince Johnson and his men forced themselves into the very room where General Quinoo and Doe were meeting. The Executive Mansion Guards, highly trained Special Forces, attempted to retrieve their weapons and fight back. Prince Johnson's forces overwhelmed them and killed most of the Executive Mansion Guards. In the firefight, Prince Johnson's men shot Doe in the leg and captured him as well as some of his guards.

This INPFL victory provided the much sought after opportunity for the Gio/Mano tribes to avenge the previous killing of Quiwonkpa and other Nimbians (those from Nimba County). The documented torture and killing of Doe that followed his capture is a continuation of the intertribal conflicts and ethnic divisiveness that has characterized the history of Liberia. Those ethnic allegiances manifested themselves in the multiple factions that fought during the Civil War.

As a student of the history of Liberia and as a survivor of its dark and brutal Civil War, I have learned much about the role of tribal and ethnic allegiance. One observation I have is that some people view themselves more as part of a tribal group than as a member of a nation. That type of loyalty taken too far results in narrow and rigid thinking that is a detriment to the society. History conveys that too much self-interest does not foster good citizenship. The Bible reveals the folly of focusing on our own desires: "What causes fights and quarrels among you? Don't they come from your desires that battle within you?" (James 4:1).

The various fighting factions involved in the Civil War in Liberia thrust our society into national confusion and forced the separation of many families, including my own. Many sought refuge in an effort to survive, and survival required navigating through the troubled waters of conflict based to a large extent on ethnic identity.

References
(Chapter Four)

Angie Elisabeth Brooks-Randolph. (n.d.). *Encyclopædia Britannica*. Retrieved from http://www.britannica.com/EBchecked/topic/1359947/Angie-Elisabeth-Brooks-Randolph

Liberia. (2014). *Online Etymology Dictionary*. Retrieved from http://www.etymonline.com

Liberia gains independence. (2013). *African American Registry*. Retrieved from http://www.aaregistry.org/historic_events/view/liberia-gains-independence

National July 26 oration: "In national unity we will stand," Father Robert Tikpor (2010, July). Retrieved from http://www.theliberian-journal.com/index.php?st=news&sbst=details&rid=1598

The lone star: The story of Liberia. (2002). Retrieved from http://www.pbs.org/wgbh/globalconnections/liberia/essays/history/

CHAPTER FIVE

TO THE BAMBAGIDA HIGHWAY

The warning from Emmanuel's auntie to be careful remained on our minds as Pekin John and I gathered what few belongings we had and prepared to leave the Iron Factory community. We prepared to leave with Emmanuel and his brother Timothy, who was my age, a few years younger than his older brother Emmanuel. We had decided to go to the Ricks Institute campus in an area called Virginia. The Ricks Institute was a co-ed boarding school where Emmanuel and Timothy had attended high school. (Interestingly, Charles Taylor had attended and graduated from the Ricks Institute years previously.) Emmanuel had gotten food there several days before we arrived at his auntie's house, and we thought food would still be available.

As we left that day around 11:00 a.m., we could still hear fighting between the INPFL and the AFL soldiers in the swamp. Walking away from the house on a dusty road, we occasionally ducked as we heard bullets flying above us. We continued to walk away, taking the same Freeway Road that we had followed on our way in. Moving farther from the Iron Factory community and the swamp area, we heard fewer gunshots and bullets in the air. Again, the Lord's grace was faithful and delivered us from this combat area. We later learned that many were killed in the Iron Factory community as a result of the fighting there between the INPFL and the AFL.

The four of us followed the Freeway Road until it intersected with Jamaica Road. At that junction we left the road due to the increased

INPFL activity we saw and wanted to avoid. After leaving the road, we passed between buildings, zigzagging our way toward the Ricks Institute. We stayed off main roads until we got to Logan Town. At Logan Town, we had to get onto the main road to get to the Ricks Institute. After getting on the main road, we saw an INPFL checkpoint that we would have to go through.

Many people of all ages were on the main road. Some carried their clothes and other belongings on their heads. Among the thousands of people, there was movement in all directions. Some were fleeing fighting in Monrovia, others were in search of food, and others were heading to areas beyond Bushrod Island controlled by Charles Taylor's forces (NPFL). Those leaving the island did so mainly because they had relatives in other areas. Regardless of where they were going, the civilians had to pass through checkpoints where heavily armed soldiers questioned them and asked for identification.

When we got to the checkpoint we fell in line with a group of men. We approached a soldier whose bullet straps crisscrossed under the red scarf that identified him as a member of the INPFL. He held a large-caliber automatic gun. We advanced toward him until he suddenly yelled, "Halt." We stopped and immediately a couple of shots rang out loudly. All of us dove to the ground. We thought we were to be killed. After a few moments of confusion, we realized that he only fired a couple of shots. We looked around as we lay on the ground and knew that no one had been killed. Then he said, "Get up." As we rose to our feet, he asked, "Where are you from?"

Emmanuel, the oldest among us, replied: "We're coming from the Iron Factory community, and we're going to the Ricks Institute to look for food."

"Is that true," asked the soldier as he looked at each of us. We all nodded and said yes. He laughed at us and told us to go. He pointed out the direction we had to take as we passed through the checkpoint; those passing through could only walk on one side of the road. In the distance, we saw another checkpoint.

As we walked on, we realized that the soldier had fired his weapon into the air suddenly to see how we would react. The checkpoints controlled by the INPFL were set up mainly to identify men or boys who had combat experience either with the AFL soldiers loyal to Doe or with Taylor's NPFL. Those with combat experience would have reacted differently from us because they would not have been as frightened. Any men or boys suspected of having combat experience were inspected for signs of soldiering. Their hands and shoulders were inspected for signs of holding or carrying arms. Their lower legs were examined for evidence of wearing boots. The men or boys with combat experience willing to join the INPFL were taken to the base for retraining and use by the INPFL. Any with combat experience who resisted were taken to the INPFL base for execution.

An interesting thing happened when we had moved far enough away from the INPFL checkpoint to feel safe. Even though he was the youngest person in our group, Pekin John decided to have some fun with us. As we talked about going through the checkpoint, Pekin John showed some of his self-confident side. He started to act as if he had not been afraid, and he began describing how scared the rest of us were. Talking about the incident and describing how scared we acted wasn't enough, however, for Pekin John.

He then proceeded to demonstrate to the rest of us how we acted as he imitated us by shaking in fear and dropping helplessly to the ground. We couldn't help but laugh at him as depicted how brave he had been and how cowardly we had acted. That led all of us to start joking with one another as we each claimed that we were the bravest. I remember Timothy, pulling on my shirt and saying, "You were afraid, not so?" I smiled back at him and responded, "You were afraid also, not so?" That humorous incident was over far too quickly because as we walked we advanced closer to the next checkpoint where our claims of bravery would be tested by armed strangers.

By the time we made it to the next checkpoint in the Point Four area, it was early afternoon, about 2:00 p.m. We had nothing to eat or drink; fortunately, the day was not unbearably hot and it had rained some. The road was crowded as usual with people moving in all directions. We approached the checkpoint, falling in line with the people heading north as we were. We stepped closer and closer in the line that was about three people wide. Eventually, we were close enough for an armed soldier to approach us. The one who moved toward us was a light-skinned mulatto.

As the soldier approached us, he and Emmanuel made eye contact and Emmanuel realized that the soldier had been one of his classmates in middle school in Bassa Community. Emmanuel called his name and the solider recognized him. They shook hands and all of us relaxed. Because he had not seen the former classmate in many years, Emmanuel asked where he had been all that time. The soldier replied that he had joined the NPFL initially and had gone to Cote d'Ivoire and Burkina Faso for military training. Later, when the NPFL split, he had joined the INPFL, headed by Prince Johnson. In response to the soldier asking where we were going, Emmanuel explained that we were headed to the Ricks Institute in search of food. The soldier told us the best route to take, which was off the main road. After he shook hands with all of us, we proceeded through the checkpoint.

As we walked, we talked briefly about how blessed we had been to see Emmanuel's former classmate at the checkpoint. We felt good inside to know that we knew one of the soldiers. The soldier had expressed to us briefly how the INPFL was not interested in mistreating civilians. Instead, the INPFL seemed to want to protect civilians. Seeing Emmanuel's former classmate at the checkpoint boosted our morale and gave us a sense of confidence. Knowing that the Lord was with us and had been leading us on our journey gave us a feeling of peace.

Taking the advice of the Emmanuel's former classmate, we left the main road and went through a community called New Kru Town. From there we eventually merged back onto the main road and followed it into Duala. Although we were now on the northernmost side of Bushrod Island and near the St. Paul River Bridge, there were still throngs of people on the road. Some were heading south into the area we were leaving, but most were heading across the St. Paul River into an area that for the most part was not tightly controlled by any military forces.

Escaping from rebel forces

At the St. Paul River Bridge, we faced our last checkpoint before leaving Bushrod Island. Although Taylor's NPFL forces were too far north in Bomi County at that time to pose a threat to the bridge, the INPFL guarded it cautiously, knowing the St. Paul River Bridge was a strategic location and a northern gateway to Bushrod Island. Because there were actually two bridges across the river, an old and a new one, the INPFL blocked the new one with their military vehicles. Standing on the new bridge, the soldiers watched the pedestrian traffic that was allowed to cross on the older bridge. Because we were leaving Bushrod Island and the territory under the control of the INPFL, we did not have to answer questions or show identification to cross the bridge. Those entering Bushrod Island from Bomi and Montserrado counties faced more questioning.

Passing through Brewerville, we tried to visit Pastor Toby Gbeh who was a pastor of St. Simon Baptist Church in Bassa Community, the church where we had gathered for prayer meetings prior to the conflict breaking out in Monrovia. We located his wife and children at the Lott Carey Baptist Mission School in Brewerville. Pastor Gbeh taught at the mission school in addition to his pastoral work. At the time, however, he was not present; his wife informed us that he was traveling. After asking us about our destination, we told her about our plans to go to Ricks Institute. She thought that was a good plan. She also expressed concern about running out of food at their mission.

From Brewerville, we only had to walk about an hour or so along the Bambagida Highway, a road named after a former Nigerian president, to get to the Ricks Institute. Both sides of the paved road were crowded with people. Occasionally an INPFL military vehicle would speed by, but there was little traffic apart from pedestrians. The sides of the road were littered with plastic bags and discarded sections of sugar cane that people chewed on as they walked. When we saw others with multiple sections of sugar cane, we asked them to share and they usually did. Apart from chewing on sugar cane, we had nothing else to eat between the Iron Factory community and the Ricks Institute.

We had left the Iron Factory community around 11:00 a.m., and we approached the gate of the Ricks Institute at about 5:00 p.m. The tall main gate faced the Bambagida Highway and was flanked by thick trees that served as a natural fence. The gate was open, so we proceeded in between the trees that lined the roadway leading through the campus. I had only visited the Ricks Institute once previously. I had attended a Baptist youth assembly meeting there for several days about three years prior.

As a boarding school, the Ricks Institute facilities were sometimes used for church-related conferences and events. The campus had buildings for teaching staff and their families, dormitories for male and female students, and multiple instructional buildings. The complex also contained recreational fields. The school usually closed in July like most other Liberian schools, but due to war the Ricks Institute as well as most other schools had closed in June. When we arrived, we joined thousands of other refuges who had fled from various parts of Liberia in an effort to escape combat areas.

Immediately after arriving, Emmanuel and Timothy, both of whom had attended school at the Ricks Institute, helped us locate the principal, Miss Grace Minor. She was glad to see her former students, and she welcomed us. We told her that we needed to stay at the Ricks Institute if possible. She said that would be okay and referred us to speak with the school administrator who could find a room for us and help us get some food. The school administrator led us to a classroom that the four of us shared. The dormitories were completely filled and had been for some time. We slept in the classroom, using the mats and some sheets that the school provided.

At first, getting enough food at the Ricks Institute was no problem. We ate rice, potato greens, and palm oil. We all enjoyed the food. For Pekin John and me, it was the best food we'd had since leaving our home in the Bassa Community on July 9, over two weeks earlier. We felt safe at the Ricks Institute and slept well on the classroom floor. The absence of gunfire at night refreshed us, enabling us to catch up on our rest.

During the days at the Ricks Institute, Pekin John played football (soccer) with some of the other youth staying on the campus. From the time he was very small, Pekin John showed strong interest and ability in football. When he was only about five, he asked our father to buy a football. Our father's investment in the football was not wasted. Pekin John played often, developing skills that he soon applied on the football team at his elementary school. He emerged as one of the best players at the school and in the league.

Watching my brother on the field at the Ricks Institute reminded me of an image that is still vivid in my mind. Pekin John's elementary school (Monrovia Demonstration Elementary) won the football league championship. Pekin John was the leading scorer. After the game, everyone in our neighborhood knew that he was the hero because of the victory parade that ended at our house. Pekin John's soccer team carried him from the field to his house above them on their outstretched hands. Followed by many others from his school, the group came singing and chanting through our neighborhood, exuberant that Pekin John had led his team to victory and was the leading scorer. At the Ricks Institute, it took very little time for others to recognize Pekin John's abilities on the football field.

After staying with us for two nights at the Ricks Institute, Emmanuel and Timothy decided they needed to return to their auntie's house at the Iron Factory community. They were able to get two partially filled 100-pound bags of rice from the Ricks Institute, one for each to carry. As they prepared to leave, we talked about our plans with Emmanuel and Timothy. Thinking the war would end quickly after President Doe was captured and ousted, we said that we would see them again soon. At the time, we hoped that we would see them again in a few weeks as we returned home through Bushrod Island. None of us had experienced war before, so we had no reason to believe that the war would last very long. We said goodbye to Emmanuel and Timothy and watched them walk away from the Ricks Institute carrying their bags of rice. Like so many other relatives and friends that we parted ways with during the war, we had no way to communicate with them and could only pray for their safety.

While staying at the Ricks Institute, we only had two ways of getting information about the war: from people who had fled conflict areas and through radio. Those who had witnessed fighting carried out by Taylor's rebel forces talked about the special powers that the rebels seemed to possess. There was talk about how the rebel soldiers could disappear and reappear. Some also believed that the rebel soldiers could be shot but not harmed due to their powers. Other reports focused on the INPFL forces and Prince Johnson's silver pistol. The rumor was that periodically INPFL commander Prince Johnson would personally carry out executions. Reasons for execution included mistreatment of others or stealing. Among those executed were INPFL soldiers, enemy soldiers, or civilians. According to the rumor, Prince Johnson carried out executions by removing his silver pistol from his holster and singing as he shot the perpetrator. Those reports generated great fear among the civilians.

Each morning we listened to the radio, especially to a news program called "Focus on Africa" broadcast by the BBC. That program provided more reliable and accurate information about the war in Liberia than local and national radio programs. At that time, Charles Taylor's NPFL controlled a major radio station (Liberia Radio Network) and President Samuel Doe controlled the government radio station (ELBC). One morning we heard by radio about a massacre at St. Peter's Lutheran Church, located on Tubman Boulevard in Monrovia.

Many people, especially those of the Gio and Mano tribes, had sought refuge at the church, thinking that the church would be safe from fighting. I knew some individuals who planned to take refuge in St. Peter's Lutheran Church on Tubman Boulevard in the Sinkor area of Monrovia. I considered going there also, but I chose not to.

As it turned out, approximately 900 people, including women and children, sought shelter at St. Peter's Lutheran Church. Those individuals did not think that soldiers would harm them there. Unfortunately, in July 1990, soldiers from the AFL committed a brutal massacre at the church. Later reports from the incident indicated that approximately 600 innocent civilians including women and children were killed in the massacre. Those killed in the church massacre were mainly Gios and Manos who were murdered by the Krahn forces of the AFL. Reports of the massacre and the church windows that were stained with blood forced us all to face the reality of the severity of war.

Apparently, one reason for the massacre at St. Peter's Lutheran Church was to convince potential soldiers not to join the NPFL rebels under the leadership of Charles Taylor. Taylor's own father was among those killed in the massacre. From that time forward we knew that no place would be safe in the escalating conflict.

When I heard the news, I remembered that the church where the massacre occurred was a place we had considered going for safety. It was the Lord that kept us from going there or we would have been among those men, women, and children who were killed. Combined with reports shared by others, the radio news about the massacre at the church deeply affected all of us, and we realized the depths to which our nation had plummeted. We had to adjust to new depths of violence and disregard for human life and social institutions.

After we had been at the Ricks Institute for little over a week, the thousands of people taking refuge there began to realize that the food supply was running low. The principal, Miss Grace Minor, asked the heads of families staying at the institute to assemble for an important message. In the school hall, the principal announced that the institute was running out of food. People were welcome to stay at the Ricks Institute, but the food would be rationed until it ran out. Then those who wanted to could stay at the institute, but they would have to find food on their own. This message was delivered just a couple of days before July 26.

July 26 is important in that it is Liberia's Independence Holiday. Due to the holiday, more people than normal listened to the radio. Perhaps that is why two important addresses were delivered via radio on July 26, 1990.

One of the speakers was Ellen Johnson Sirleaf, who at that time supported Taylor's NPFL. She stated that NPFL forces were already in Monrovia and planned to take over the executive mansion. Sirleaf indicated that President Doe had stated his intention not to surrender until the last man in his army died. According to Sirleaf, in an effort to minimize casualties the NPFL would destroy the executive mansion if needed in order to overthrow Doe. That approach was designed, she explained, to shorten the conflict. The executive mansion could be rebuilt if it was destroyed, but the loss of life could not be replaced.

The other radio address was from Charles Taylor himself. Taylor stated that the NPFL had ordered Doe to step down and leave the country. In conjunction with the American government, arrangements had been made for Doe to leave Liberia and go to Nigeria. This arrangement was communicated as representing the best interests of the people and would minimize war casualties. Taylor reported, however, that Doe refused to leave because he was elected by the people and the NPFL had no right to order him to leave. Taylor stated that he wanted to fight but that the international community pressured him to allow civilians to leave before widespread fighting broke out. Therefore, Taylor stated that he would open the Bambagida Highway leading to Sierra Leone. That highway was the designated corridor for civilians to use to leave the country before the conflict intensified. Taylor warned that any that remained did so at their own risk.

Shortly after the radio announcements on July 26, we had to leave the Ricks Institute due to the food shortage. We knew of some friends who had left Monrovia to stay with their uncle on a cassava farm near the Ricks Institute. We stayed with them for several days, knowing that we could get food there. Also, the location gave us the opportunity to question those taking the Bambagida Highway to Sierra Leone. By talking with those on the highway, we could get news from Monrovia and we could make sure that Taylor's announcement was not a trap. We quickly learned that the situation in Monrovia was deteriorating and that going back there was not an option. We also gained confidence that use of the Bambagida Highway was fairly safe. We did not see those passing returning, and that added to our confidence.

We stayed with our friends' uncle at the cassava farm for about three days. We had to steal cassava to have food to eat. There was little control or accountability due to the vast numbers of hungry people. During our three days' stay, Pekin John was quite sick with malaria. With no medicine available, all Pekin John could do was take a drink made from boiled bitter leaves that was supposed to clear one's system. Shortly thereafter, he became stronger. Little food was left at the cassava farm, and we knew that we had to move on.

Each day more and more people passed on their way to Sierra Leone. At that point, I told Pekin John that we had to leave and take the Bambagida Highway to Sierra Leone. The next day we told our friends goodbye. They told us that we would not survive because the route to Sierra Leone led directly through the stronghold of Taylor's forces. Regardless of the advice from our friends, we really had no option but to head to Sierra Leone.

CHAPTER SIX

PREPARATION FOR PROMOTION: MY EDUCATION

As the crisis of war escalated, forcing Pekin John and me to leave on a treacherous journey to Sierra Leone, I experienced many emotions. Difficult times are often a catalyst for thinking about values and purpose. During the time that Pekin John and I prepared to leave our native Liberia, the reality of war affected me deeply. I began to reflect on my life, and—perhaps from the security associated with memories from peaceful times—I began to think about how much I appreciated the role of education in my life.

Before I started school, my father taught my brothers and sisters and me at home for one year. I was taught the 26 letters of the alphabet, numbers from 1 to 20 and two-letter words such as "go, lo, and no." I remember writing the letter E with five legs instead of three. I received my kindergarten and part of my elementary education at the Pilgrim Foundation School from 1972 – 1977 located in the Bassa community area, near the national police headquarters.

At this school I was double promoted from Premier I to first grade and from first grade to third grade. I finished the fourth grade at Pilgrim Foundation School and graduated with honors. I then attended the Kazier Kollie Elementary School which was located in the Buzzi/Lorma Quarter area and was also a government school (called public school in other countries). It was near one of the popular streets in Monrovia called Camp Johnson Road.

At Kazier Kollie Elementary School, I completed fifth and sixth Grades from 1978-1979. I was at the top of my class and also served as president of the school for the student council. I was elected as President of the student council through students' elections conducted by the administration of the school. Another student and I were the two students who contested for the position to represent our fellow students in case of problems or issues affecting the school. I won over my friend John Kollie to become the president of the student council. After the elections I was inducted into office along with fellow students who were appointed to serve in various capacities.

In 1980 I enrolled at the Bassa Teenage Junior High School and completed seventh through ninth Grades. This middle public school ran classes from seventh grade to ninth grade. The uniform for this school was a yellow shirt with navy blue trousers. This school also offered vocational training for students who felt inclined to offer one of the vocational courses in the future as a career. I also enrolled in one of the vocational courses and studied electricity. This school is located in the Bassa Community and is presently called the Bassa Community Academy. I served there as Secretary General and President for my class and my school. I completed ninth grade as the top student in the school and with distinction as indicated on my West African Certificate Examination (WEAC).

Some of my school and classmates in Junior High School were John Vaye, Daniel Debois, Hellen Zubah, Rosaline Weah, Samuel Gbaydee Doe, Dorothea Quinae, Annie Mulbah, Jimmy Harry, Evelyn Barry, Wahib, Joe Tieh, Arthur Weay, Isaac Miller, Shelton Tarpeh, James Railey, Thomas Nimene and Eddie Verdier. I treasure the memories of those individuals, some of whom are no longer living.

For extracurricular activities, I took part in the Lawana Christian Fellowship, an outreach of the Scripture Union of Liberia. In this fellowship, we all participated in the Inter-Junior High School Quiz Competition. We recited Bible memorization and answered questions on Bible knowledge. This competition took place in the Monrovia City Hall and was aired over Radio ELWA.

I became the top quizzer from all the junior high schools in Liberia in 1982. As a result, I was given a scholarship to attend the school of my choice. By 1983, I received a scholarship and attended the Booker T. Washington Institute in Kakata, Margibi County. Before attending the Booker T. Washington Institute, I was also offered a scholarship by Suehn Mission, Lower Bopolu, but my choice was the Institute. I attended the Institute for a while, but following a student riot, I returned to Monrovia. By July, I enrolled at the R.C. Lawson High School. My attendance there was supported also by a scholarship.

I was also active in student politics. I became a member and Secretary General of the Voice of the Students Party. For my Senior High, or secondary education, I studied Electricity as a vocational course. Since I was there on scholarship, I was a member of the Quiz Team. The Teen Time quiz was a students' event organized by the Youth of Christ of Liberia (YFC) in collaboration with the Eternal Love Winning Africa (ELWA), a radio station owned by the Sudan Interior Mission (SIM). Each school contesting was given books from the Holy Bible to study and questions were asked and four students represented their school and the first student to stand when the question was asked was to complete the question and give the answer. Any student who answered five questions correctly was given a bonus and had to leave the team to be substituted. Students who answered the highest number of questions during the year received a scholarship to attend any school of their choice.

In July of 1983, there was a students' riot on the campus and the government closed down the school. The riot came about as a result of students not getting the food and assistance that the government had given to the school authorities. The living condition on the campus was not conducive and teachers were not teaching regularly as they were supposed to. The students' leadership kept negotiating with the administration of the school but there was no progress. Things were getting worse, and as a result the Students Council called a meeting for all students to riot against the school administration. During this riot the students' leaders caught the principal and other authorities of the schools and beat them. Others were locked up in the school toilets and stayed there the whole day. This riot was brought to an end when the then Vice Head of State under the Peoples' Redemption Council, Brg. J. Nicholas Podier, sent military men to put the riot under control and called a general meeting of students and school administration to announce closure of the school indefinitely.

Because of my quest to complete high school on time, I returned to Monrovia and enrolled at the R.C. Lawson Institute where I completed the Tenth Grade, or Form 4. God was good to me and I received another scholarship to Haywood Mission School where I completed Eleventh and Twelfth Grades, or Form 5 and 6. I also served on the Student Council as Advisor and graduated in December of 1985 as the Valedictorian of the school.

My valedictorian speech was titled, "Education is the Bridge to Success." In this speech I mentioned firstly how there was a vast gap between those who have and those who do not have. I quoted from Oliver Wendell Holmes who said, "The main part of intellectual education is not

the acquisition of facts but learning how to make facts live." I emphasized that every calling is great when greatly pursued and that there was
not equal desire of education, but there was not equal access to achieve
education, needless to say quality education, due to this big gap. I also
drew from another quotation from Holmes that stated, "It's faith in something and enthusiasm for something that makes a life worth living" and
that as humans "the great thing in the world is not where we stand, but in
what direction we are moving." What could bridge this gap was having
EDUCATION. Having an education could provide a level playing field
for all.

Other elements of my valedictory address included the quotation
"Tell me and I'll forget; show me and I may remember: involve me and
I'll understand." I shared the statement, "The object of education is to
prepare the young to educate themselves throughout their lives." I also
said that through education—if the opportunity is given to any one from
both backgrounds—he or she could succeed. I stated, "Too often students
are given answers to remember, rather than problems to solve."

My valedictory speech concluded by emphasizing that success will
not come easily but will come as a result of seriousness and commitment to study and desire to pass your exams and tests. The final quote
I shared was "Education of the mind without educating the heart is no
education at all."

Since the requirement of the West African Examination Council
(WAEC) was to pass all subjects in WAEC and in your school, many students did not qualify for graduation. Those of us who passed represented
only seven of fifty students from our school. It was painful and difficult
to look at the faces of my friends when we showed up at the school for
our results. It was a feeling of joy and sorrow. Some of our friends cried
and stood up for a long time and gazed at the sky as if they were praying
to the Lord to change the results automatically before the day of graduation. That year it was not just in our school that students did not do well;
many students around the country and in West Africa did not do well in
the examinations.

In March of 1986, I sat for the entrance examination to the University
of Liberia (UL). I passed the exam and enrolled at the UL in July of
1986. At the UL, I studied zoology and chemistry at the T.J.R. Faulkner
College of Science and Technology on the Fendell Campus. My dream
was to become a medical doctor. Therefore, I needed a bachelor of science in zoology and chemistry to enroll at the A.M. Duglattis College of
Medicine. I stayed at the UL from 1986 to 1990. During my final year, I

helped conduct physics and chemistry labs for the non-science freshmen students. My ID number was 15005.

I also took part in the Student Council government. I served in the Student Unification party as a representative for the Fendell campus. In the elections for this position during my sophomore year, I won by a landslide victory over a junior student. I also served as the Secretary General of the Biology Students Association and the Rivercess Students Association. During the year that I served as Secretary General in 1988, we took a team of students from this association to Cesstos, Rivercess County, to help all the senior high school students that were sitting for the West African Certificate Exams (WAEC) that year. Each year the Biology Students Association (BIOSA) organized sports and we played against other student associations and then prepared food and ate and fellow-shipped together. At that time, Mary Antionette Brown Sherman was the Dean of the Science College and the Vice President was Dr. Wilson Tarpeh.

Some of my lecturers were Prof. Frederick Hunter, Dr. Jacob Matior, and Dr. Thomas from India and also Dr. Kekualah, Prof. Ward, Dr. Wreh, Dr. E. Harmon, etc. One of the most difficult courses was organic chemistry. Any student who failed Chemistry 301 and 302 could not continue to the medical college. To pass this course we slept at the Agricultural College for days sometimes without taking a bath and stayed up late at night studying. Passing was a great victory for many students. As I recall, many of the students were frustrated by Prof. Ward who was the main lecturer.

Education is very important to me. The right and positive information produces knowledge and knowledge produces power. There are positive and negative powers in education. If education is used positively, it leads to promotion. Education occurs from the cradle to the grave.

For me, to stop learning is to stop leading. All I know is all that I have learned. Therefore, I must gain knowledge. Ignorance is a state of lacking knowledge or education. Every day of my life should be an opportunity to learn (II Timothy 2:15 and Psalm 119:130).

Education is preparation for promotion. Everything we have learned and will learn is not in vain. Every fact we learn is a stepping-stone, or the platform to promotion.

In I Samuel 17:34–37, we see how David, though young, prepared himself for promotion. He killed the bears and the lions to protect the sheep. This preparation in the wilderness gave him the courage to kill Goliath. This resulted in David's promotion.

In Genesis 39:20–23, we read about Joseph's preparation in the prison. He studied Egyptian customs, their political system, their history and their language. When opportunity came for promotion, Joseph was the chosen one. He became Prime Minister of Egypt.

In Daniel 1:8–21, we read how Daniel refused to defile himself with the royal food. Instead of the rich diet, he ate healthy food to remain physically strong. When he appeared before the kings, he was immediately chosen to serve on the king's staff.

Failure to prepare is preparation to fail. It is said that information produces knowledge and knowledge produces power. There is no success story that is not rooted in information. Success depends on how much information one has and what is done with it (I Corinthians 12:32).

In my final year at the University of Liberia, the war that started in December of 1989 came to the capital city. This forced the university to close down on June 4, 1990, and forced me to stop serving as a Sunday School teacher at my local church. My dream of becoming a medical doctor found no other option except to be deferred. The closing of the University of Liberia was one the most difficult realities that I had ever faced. Reflecting on it now remains very painful. My opportunity to complete the studies required to become a medical doctor was ripped from me. I was discouraged and disappointed.

CHAPTER SEVEN

THE ROAD TO SURVIVAL

I n his book *Things Fall Apart,* Chinua Achebe wrote ". . . mere anarchy is loosed upon the world." That quote describes the situation in Liberia when there was a government—under Doe's presidency—that had no control. With the loss of authority there was lawlessness and chaos. Many people ran in all directions looking for hideouts in churches, government buildings, and abandoned buildings where they thought they would be safe from rebels or soldiers. It was under those circumstances that Pekin John and I took the Bambagida highway toward Sierra Leone, despite the warnings from our friends that we would not survive.

As a result of the previous radio announcements by Charles Taylor stating that the Bambagida highway to Sierra Leone was open, many thousands of people used the road as their escape route from escalating violence in Liberia. Like before, when Pekin John and I had traveled on the road to the Rick's Institute, the highway was filled with litter from the many civilians fleeing on foot. This time, however, the number of people was much greater. Glancing ahead, we felt as if we were looking across an ocean of people. Most people carried few items with them, hauling what little they had on lappas tied and resting atop heads. Others tried to carry too much, using wheelbarrows in an effort to preserve as many of their belongings as possible. All that Pekin John and I carried was one plastic bag each. As we looked across the Bambagida highway, we could see men, women, and children, all hoping to find refuge in Sierra Leone.

The journey to Sierra Leone was the second time in my life that I had moved to a new place to live. The first trip was my family's move when I was four years old. We walked from our village to Charlie's Town to get a public transport to travel to Monrovia. That journey had been exciting. I was able to experience riding in a vehicle for the first time, seeing the many beautiful buildings, lights, and paved roads of Monrovia, and I had the opportunity to drink soda (Coca Cola) for the first time.

Unlike that trip 19 years previous that was filled with excitement and expectations, it was much different when Pekin John and I walked on the road leading to Sierra Leone. There was fear, sadness, and uncertainty everywhere. There was uncertainty because we did not know what was ahead of us and things could change quickly. We could be walking and just out of the blue a rebel could appear and shout at everyone to stop. They could search us and ask several questions. If the answers did not satisfy them, they were quick to execute on the spot. Dead bodies were all over the roads, and the trees and bushes were extremely quiet, seemingly pregnant with soldiers ready to burst forth and attack. No one trusted the next person. Who could know their agenda and where they were from and who they were supporting? Most of the time, we walked without talking. This made the journey more boring and caused us to be more fearful.

Although many people wanted to find safety in Sierra Leone, scores never completed the journey. Few of the people who carried many possessions were able to reach their destination. Carrying too many items attracted attention from others, including rebels who desired to take any possessions they could, even if it meant killing to get what they wanted. Others got sick on the way to Sierra Leone and could proceed no further. Many suffered from swollen legs or feet due to the long distance walking. Those who were overweight had to deal with chafed skin from their legs rubbing against each other with no opportunity to change clothes. Because our journey to Sierra Leone occurred during the rainy season, the weather negatively affected everyone. After sundown, those traveling on the road had to stop in the darkness and lie down to sleep on the side of the road. Sometimes the rain poured steadily throughout the night on those who had no change of clothes, no shelter for sleeping, and no food. Whether due to fatigue, illness, violence, or hunger, many never found the safety they sought.

Along the way to Sierra Leone, a regular source of food was not available. Our staple foods included rice, cassava, potatoes, yams, and meat (chicken, beef, sheep, or goat). Those foods were not available, so we had to resort to eat raw cassava. In Liberia, cassava is such a staple that each of the various tribes has its own way of preparing it and they call it different names. For example, the Bassa tribe called it fufu and dumboy, and the Gio or Mano call it ganykpa (GB for short). In its form called farina, cassava is ground and is eaten with milk and sugar or with palm oil, salt, and pepper. Under normal circumstances cassava is not to be eaten raw. Due to the war, however, eating raw cassava was common. In the small plastic bags we carried, Pekin John and I had a limited supply of cassava.

Sugar cane, due to its abundance, was also a common food for those walking to Sierra Leone. Occasionally, we also ate sour plum, a fruit produced on some of the trees that we passed along the way. Another food eaten as a last resort was boiled potato leaves. Occasionally, someone built a fire and had a pot for boiling potato leaves. Though not very nutritious, boiled potato leaves were better than nothing.

Interacting with others in an effort to get food or resting with other travelers in abandoned buildings provided opportunities to get news about the war. Some people had portable radios that enabled them to get news via the BBC at 3:15 p.m. and 5:15 p.m. To conserve battery power, most of those with radios tuned in to the BBC program "Focus on Africa" only at those times. Reports on the radio made it clear that those who thought the conflict would end soon were mistaken. In contrast, the fighting intensified throughout Liberia and in Monrovia in particular.

Forces loyal to then president Doe, Prince Johnson, and Charles Taylor were all competing for control of the country. The coveted symbol of control was occupation of the executive mansion; for that prize the factions toiled ruthlessly. News reports revealed that Moses Duopo and Sam Dokie, both former ministers in Doe's government were killed. Both of them had joined Taylor's NPFL as senior leaders, but ideological issues reportedly brought division between them and other leaders within the NPFL. Similarly, Jackson Doe, who ran in the presidential elections against Samuel Doe in 1985, was killed after joining the NPFL. According to the BBC, there was speculation by international observers that Jackson Doe had actually won the 1985 presidential election but that the election had been rigged. News of the deaths of three prominent former government leaders who had joined the NPFL sent a message that the violence was escalating.

Beyond the news reports through radio, another event signaled the progression of war. After two days of walking on the Bambagida highway toward Sierra Leone, we came to a big town called Sasstown. This was a big market area during normal time, but there were not many people there when we arrived. While we were walking in Sasstown between the huge piles of trash that lined that area near the market, we saw several cars pass us. We recognized some of the vehicles and some of those who were in them. In one of the cars was Rev. Momolu Diggs, pastor of the oldest church in Liberia, Providence Baptist Church. His family was with him. Also, we recognized Rev. David Daniels, pastor of the Elizer Turner Memorial AME church, and his family. There were others we did not recognize, but I thought they were church leaders or senior citizens.

Seeing those well-known and respected church leaders fleeing toward Sierra Leone convinced me that things had gotten worse in Monrovia. Those leaders along with others from the Liberia Council of Churches had marched in Monrovia in April of 1990 in an effort to keep war from coming to Monrovia. They had given speeches and had asked for the resignation of President Doe so that the war could end before it reached Monrovia and resulted in the killing of more citizens and destruction of properties. Their appeals for Doe to resign had been answered with firm resistance. At St. Peter's Lutheran Church, a number of innocent civilians were killed. Most of those had been from Nimba County. Months later, it was clear that those well respected church leaders fled for fear of losing their lives.

From Sasstown, we walked on toward Klay Junction, an intersection where the Bambagida highway turned sharply to the left and another road continued north toward Klay. As we approached Klay Junction, we saw for the first time Taylor's NPFL rebels. Unlike the INPFL rebels, who were dressed in military uniforms and were easily recognizable by their red scarves, the NPFL rebels did not wear uniforms. Their commanders wore military uniforms and red berets, but the rebels looked like civilians with the exception of the weapons they carried. Most of the rebels carried AK-47s; some had rifles; some had M203s (grenade launchers). Those who did not have guns carried knives and/or machetes. As we observed the heavily armed rebels, we were overtaken by fear and remembered the warnings from those who had said that we would not make it through the stronghold of Taylor's forces.

We had seen AFL soldiers in their military uniforms, and we had seen INPFL rebels in their military uniforms. In both cases, there seemed to be a sense of military order. Seeing the NPFL rebels in their plain clothes instilled greater fear because they appeared to be civilians recklessly playing with guns, eager to shoot at civilian targets who displayed the slightest sign of resistance. Also, the many reports of the seemingly magical powers of the NPFL rebels affected all who had heard the accounts of the rebels disappearing and reappearing. As Pekin John and I approached the checkpoint at Klay Junction, we were aware of the danger we faced. We said nothing to each other due in part to the shock of seeing the rebels for the first time. In my heart, I prayed that God would enable us to pass through the NPFL checkpoint.

We stood in line, waiting for our turn at the checkpoint. Those traveling together as a family or with others advanced together. The family ahead of us was questioned and then allowed to pass through. Then, the rebel who would question us called for us to step forward. We did so, keenly aware of the many armed rebels who were stationed all around the checkpoint watching what was happening. I can still picture the rebel who motioned us forward. He had on a long dark brown coat, like those worn in the winter in the USA, and black gloves. He asked who we were and where we were going. I told him that John and I were brothers and that we were traveling to Sierra Leone. He said that he did not believe me and claimed that I was part of the Krahn tribe. Next, he told John to go forward and not to look behind. The rebel then put his gun to my head and said that he would kill me because I was lying. I told him that I was telling the truth. Then he took the bullet out of his rifle and held it up in front of my face and said, "This is the bullet that I will use to kill you." He reloaded the gun and put the end of the barrel near my head, getting ready to shoot.

Suddenly, another rebel came running and shouted, "Do not shoot!" The rebel moved his finger from the trigger, lowered the gun, and listened to the one who came running. During that time, many things ran through my mind and I felt many things in my heart. I remembered lying under my bed and praying for God to deliver me. I thought in my heart, "God, you will not allow me to be killed."

The other rebel asked me where I came from. I told him. He then asked for my name and my tribe. At that time, I told him that I was Bassa. To prove that I was, he greeted me in Bassa and then began asking questions in Bassa. I responded to all of his questions including questions about where I was from and who my people were. Convinced that I was a member of the Bassa tribe and knowing that I was originally from Rivercess County, he turned to the rebel who was going to shoot me and said, "When we passed through Rivercess County, the Bassa people were good to us." Then he told me to go.

At Klay junction, I was arrested by the National Patriotic Front rebels because of my name, *Menyongar,* which was recognized as a family in the Liberian government. My cousin, David was a senator for Margibi County in Liberia. Because my brother was very young, the rebels directed him to leave the area. They told him to leave to not see how I would be executed.

He left crying, not knowing where he would go and who would take care of him if anything happened to me.

While the rebels were planning to kill me, another rebel came running and told them to stop. The rebel already had a bullet in the gun ready to kill me when the second man asked, "Where are you from?" I replied, "Rivercess County." He instructed the man, "Don't touch him. When we passed through their county, they were good to us." I am convinced and persuaded that this was God's doing *because He has a purpose for me.*

After this incident I my emotions overcame me when I reached Pekin John after I had been miraculously released. We shared many tears of joy and rejoiced for the great deliverance of God. The Lord had delivered us again. This turn of events was clearly His grace that is sufficient for all of us and that is unmerited. I turned and saw my younger brother with tears running down his cheeks. We both sincerely thanked the Lord for his goodness and mercy.

When we left this checkpoint we were very hungry and tired but kept walking. Shortly after we left Klay Junction, I briefly saw one of my college mates who used to preach on the students' bus when it was en route to the Fendell campus. His name was Victor McGodman, and he was walking with his auntie to Sierra Leone. After walking for about ten miles, we stopped at one of the villages near the main road where we asked to sleep for that night. These were Gola/Vai people and we asked them for water to drink but they never gave us any. This reminded me that those who live in that part of Liberia do not give water to a stranger. Indeed this rumor that circulated concerning those people proved to be true. We did not receive any water. We walked on a few more miles and slept that night in another hut near the road, almost a dirt floor with just a mattress. On that night I remembered the mattress at our house where we normally slept. It was comfortable but due to war there we were sleeping on a mat on a dirt floor. That night we ate some cassava that our friends had provided.

We, along with thousands of others, continued walking toward the Sierra Leone border. Rebels jumped out of the bush occasionally and instructed us to walk in a straight line. We continued on for two days and reached the town of Gbah. This was a strategic town for the rebels. Here we were given strict instructions not to laugh or steal. Anyone caught offending, would be killed immediately. A tall fellow stole another's sneakers. He was taken to the double bridge known as Lofa Bridge and executed in front of all of us. We stayed at Gbah for three days. When we arrived we were asked to register where we came from, questioned about our parents, and were asked to declare what we were doing.

During the registration process one of the NPFL fighters/soldiers recognized Pekin John as a footballer and because of this he found a place for us to stay and gave us ten cups of rice and palm oil. That night it was a joyous moment for us to have seen rice after so many days after we left our friends near Ricks Institute. We cooked and while eating I was so hungry that I ate and the rice came to my throat, and it was difficult for me to sleep that night. It took long for the food to digest because I was full beyond capacity. John laughed at me so much until I joined him and began to laugh at myself also. We were among rebels but because of the food we could rejoice and have some fun for a few moments.

The next morning when we woke up, we heard that a former Minister of Justice in Doe's government was scheduled to visit that place. His name was Chea Cheapoo, and he had left the government because of the activities that were going on that led to the war. He was very popular with the masses and even the rebels. Everyone was anxious to see him. He was an intriguing and controversial politician who was difficult to understand.

At this same time there were some Fulas (nomadic people who came from Guinea and lived in Liberia) whose main work was to sell or trade by opening small shops or a minimarket on the side of the road. They were also noted for roasting beef on the side of the streets in Monrovia. These men and women were trying to leave the country to go back to Guinea when they passed through Gbah. Because they were not involved in the politics of Liberia, the rebels were not concerned so much about them as compared to the Mandingoes from Guinea who were so much in the day-to-day politics of Liberia.

The rebels caught the Fulas, especially the men and put us civilians in a circle and told the men to dance. The Fulanis are noted for dancing, especially when a president from another country came to visit Liberia. The men wore big, white and red baggy pants and danced well, so they were asked to dance. The rebels told those of us watching not to laugh and that if any of us laughed we would be killed immediately. This was a very funny dance and the rebels knew that it would cause people to laugh and we believed they did this to justify their killing. If anyone was to laugh they would kill that person and tell the rest, "We told you not to laugh and this is why we killed him." But how can you tell somebody to do something that is so funny and them tell those looking on not to laugh? This was the situation we had live to with during the war. Fortunately for all of us, among the more than a hundred people that had gathered no one was killed because we tightened our lips. But it was one of the most difficult moments for us to control ourselves.

We slept again for another night. A bus came, which was taken from the Lott Carey Mission by the NPFL rebels. On it was written, "WE ARE NUMBER ONE." That was the motto of Lott Carey Mission when they were in a soccer competition against another school. The rebels used the bus to transport civilians and also their own fighters. Because there were so many people who wanted to go to the next town near the border Tien, we started to fight to jump on the bus. I remembered Pekin John, and I jumped through the windows on the bus but we were beaten severely by one rebel called GBAH RED. He was a very fearful and wicked young man who killed people for fun and this was the name they gave him for his act of wickedness. He beat us until our backs were bleeding and told us to get down from the bus the same way we have entered and we jumped through the windows again. We were very discouraged and felt that we would not be able leave, even after we had walked so far to get there.

After the next day, the same bus came back again and at that time we were able to talk to Pekin John's friend to help us get on. He did and we got on. Riding this bus was the first time since the war entered the capital city that I got in a vehicle since June 4th when the University of Liberia closed down at the Fendell campus near Carey Burg after the rebels advanced at Bentol, the home of the late President William R. Tolbert. This bus took us to the border town of Tien, but before getting to Tien we passed through Sanjey, another big town along the Bambagida Highway.

When we got to the Tien it was difficult to cross because there were four check points. At each of the checkpoints we were expected to show a pass from the NPFL to a secretary of the NPFL stationed in an old police station. A pass was difficult to obtain—and costly. The pass needed signatures of at least four commanders and many were paying about $20 US dollars to get one pass at this time. An equivalent of $20 US dollars was about $1,000 in Liberian dollars. We did not have any money on us. I told John it looked like we would not cross and that we would stay there and wait to see what the Lord would do for us. We stayed in an old two-story building which was the only type in this town.

We stayed at Tien for almost a week. We were hungry and there was no food. It came to a time that I almost begged for food. There was a woman who was selling potatoes and other food stuff but since we never had money we just passed and smelled the food but could not taste the food. It was very tempting and painful. Sometimes we were so hungry, we thought we would die. At such a time, any food seemed enticing. I had never felt hunger like that before. I began to understand why some people forget their dignity and beg for food or money.

It was during this time of waiting that news came from the NPFL frontline that the war was getting tough between the NPFL and the AFL forces loyal to Doe on one hand and with the INPFL on the other hand. As a result they were to take all young men to their training camp to train them to go and fight for the NPFL. Hearing this caused us to be troubled and disturbed. We began to pray for the Lord to make a way for us to leave Tien before we were among those conscripted into the NPFL. I kept thinking about what I would do as a big brother and was confused. I was anxious for something to happen quickly so we could flee from Tien.

Typical child soldier, forced to kill

Then, Pekin John saw one of the passes that the rebels had destroyed and he brought it to me. He showed it to me and told me it was a sample of the pass that the NPFL rebels were using which many people had been paying money for. He said he would duplicate it and sell it for us to have money. I told him that was a dangerous idea because if he were caught by the rebels he would be killed. He assured me that he could do it and no one would know.

Soon, he sold two of the duplicated passes to two men and they crossed. Then, Pekin John sold the third one and nothing happened. Watching this plan unfold with no incidents gave me courage. Pekin John made two passes for both of us to cross. When we took it to the checkpoints the rebels allowed us to cross and never suspected what had happened. We walked very fast after we crossed the last checkpoint. We were glad to have left Tien, a stronghold of the NPFL, but we were also afraid because we knew that if our deceit had been discovered, the penalty would surely have been death.

There were no more checkpoints until we got to Bo Waterside, which was the border town between Liberia and Sierra Leone. After we arrived, the first thing we did was to look for a burned building where we could sleep. We found a big room that was empty and had a partially burned roof. We entered the room with our two plastic bags which contained all our belongings. Then we started going around asking others who had arrived before us about the area and questioned them about the latest news about crossing the border into Sierra Leone.

We were told that no one was allowed to cross the borders. Tens of thousands of people had been there waiting for several weeks. The masses of people gathered there were awaiting a signal indicating they could cross the border. We were discouraged by this information, but we were glad that we were at the border. Bo Waterside was the last stop and only a small distance separated us from the sought after peace of Sierra Leone. Immediately, we began contemplating whether there were some bypass roads that we could use in the night to escape and cross the border.

During our first night at Bo Waterside, we cooked the rice we had with us and ate and slept. The next morning we went closer to the border and saw a terrible scene. We knew the man we saw tied to a tree was a member of the Krahn tribe because he was the driver of one of our father's friends. He had been tied to a big tree naked. We saw him just before he was to be burned by the rebels. We were watching closely enough for him to see us and recognize us, but he could say nothing. Fearful of causing a problem for ourselves if we said we recognized him, we could do nothing. The horror of that incident was deeply discouraging. We continued to think about ways to escape the violence of Liberia and enter Sierra Leone.

CHAPTER EIGHT

REFUGEES IN SIERRA LEONE

Afterwe stayed at Bo Waterside for about a week, one of the commanders, Oliver Varney, finally ordered that all civilians who wanted to go to Sierra Leone be allowed to cross the border. Among the tens of thousands of people who had gathered at the border waiting to cross, many had cholera, diarrhea, or malaria. Not enough medicine was available to treat the people and some died due to illness. Again, I believe it was God who intervened for His purpose to be fulfilled.

On August 2, 1990, we walked across the Mano River Union Bridge and looked behind on the Liberian side at the scenes of desperate men, women, and children fleeing their homeland. We also noticed amid the stream of tired faces the Liberian flag. We looked back at the Liberian flag and began to cry. This was the flag we saluted every day at school when we stood and recited, "I pledge my allegiance to the flag of Liberia and to the republic for which it stands, one nation, indivisible, with liberty and justice for all." At that moment, we saw a flag that represented a nation that was divided, a nation that had no more liberty, and a torn nation where injustice was the order of the day.

We cried also because we were leaving the known to go to the unknown. We were leaving the country that we were born in—leaving parents, sisters and brothers and friends—and going to Sierra Leone. In Liberia, brothers were killing brothers. We knew we would miss our country, but we would miss our family even more. We had never lived by ourselves before.

There we were, facing a country where we knew no one. We were refugees, strangers. We were totally dependent upon the Lord to carry us through. With uncertainty and doubts and fear, we crossed the bridge into Sierra Leone. Since leaving the Bassa community on July 9, 1990, we had walked about 98 miles under the strain of conflict. The future seemed bleak. Our desire to leave the country of war and lawlessness was mingled with sorrow in our hearts for those we had to leave behind. Every now and then pictures and images were going through our minds of our parents and relatives and friends what they were going through and whether they were alive or dead.

At times I was overwhelmed by anger and hatred for the rebels and all those who caused the problems in our country. We knew that many young men and boys had been captured by the rebels and forced to be their servants. Women and girls were forced to cook for them and to serve as their sex slaves. Others were conscripted into one of the warring factions. Those who were viewed or identified as enemies were eliminated, often mercilessly. Many who tried to escape ran into ambushes and were killed either by bullet wounds or by the rebels burning the vehicles. Others died in traffic accidents because the driver was too nervous or afraid to concentrate. Some who had chosen to flee by canoes died in heavy storms due to the rainy season. Our journey to Sierra Leone had resulted in hunger, thirst, a beating, and sleeping on the ground for almost a month. We had witnessed killings and other atrocities.

Many dead bodies lay in the road

Every night it was very difficult to sleep. I had dreams of wars and other fearful dreams. I also worried about my younger brother as I did not have money to feed him and wondered what would happen to him. What would my parents say after the war if I could not take care of my brother? I was confused and each time I looked at my younger brother and thought about the potential he had, I was discouraged. We were in the middle of nowhere and did not know what would happen next.

We crossed the bridge into Sierra Leone as soon as possible because the NPFL commander said once they closed it they did not know when it would open again. The Lord gave us the opportunity to cross. After entering Sierra Leone, we stayed with other Liberians who fled during the early days of the war and were established at the border town of Sierra Leone called Gendema.

The Liberians we stayed with at Gendema had helped build a shelter they lived in that they shared with us. It was the first time in many months that my brother and I ate a real meal. That night, we slept well, not worrying about the possibility of an attack. We also bought some used clothes to have the opportunity to change the only clothes we had worn for about a month. Before leaving we met some of our friends there from the Bassa community. Those friends included Oliver Johnson, Clarence Madison, and Abraham. We stayed at Gendema for about a week before we all left together and walked from Gendema to Fairo.

Walking from Gendema to Fairo was an exciting time. The journey gave us some time to refresh ourselves after a month of continual tension and struggle. We shared some jokes on things we used to do growing up. One incident we laughed about occurred at the University of Liberia campus. We went there to look for almonds and were caught. For punishment we had to do pushups. One of our friends, Junior Monyoukaye kept counting the wrong way, and the more he counted and made mistakes the more irritated the security guard became. The security guard told us to start all over. As I recall, we did more than 150 push-ups and then they beat us before releasing us! I also remember Oliver Johnson talking about the days we used to practice in the junior choir in our church, singing the songs "Come Home" and "Burdens are Lifted at Calvary."

After three days, we walked twenty-seven miles into Sierra Leone and arrived at a place called Zimmi. Along the way, we were ill-treated by some Sierra Leoneans because of our nationality. Many Sierra Leoneans were also fearful of the war spreading into their peaceful country and they directed their fears toward us as if we were representatives of the growing threat. Many times in war innocent people are victimized for what they never created. It was disturbing and at times scary when people mistreated us. We never knew the place or anyone to go to for rescue. However, most of the people in Sierra Leone treated us well and were hospitable.

Having no money, we gave some of our shoes and clothing to a driver to take us to a town called Kenema, about eighty miles from Zimmi. He took the items and allowed us to climb on his truck. He drove us to the middle of a thick jungle near the Gola Forest, told us to get down from his truck, and informed us that because we were refugees, he would not help us. We didn't know the area or anyone around. We walked about two miles and saw some houses. We went there and introduced ourselves to the Chief of that village. We were welcomed, fed, and given hot water to take baths. They also invited us to spend the night there.

In the morning, we continued our journey until we found another vehicle that took us to Kenema. We gave the driver some of our clothes and our watches and chains. In this vehicle we were packed like sardines. We had to climb on the big tires of this truck to get into the back. More than 65 people were crammed into the back of the truck. My younger brother jumped to get into the truck. There were so many foul odors in the truck because many of those on the truck had not taken a bath for one or two weeks. The truck was also uncomfortable because it was congested and hot.

In Kenema, we stayed at Kasamba Terrace with a Mende Chief. They were all very nice to us. The first night we were given cassava leaves and rice. This was our fifth time eating rice with more ingredients since we left Monrovia in July. There were brown beans in the soup and we ate it very fast as if we have never seen food before. We shared about some of what we experienced on the way to Kenema. My brother and I were seriously sick from the food and water we had eaten and drunk along the way, and we were fatigued from the long distance we had walked. After hearing about our trip and seeing our condition, some caring individuals took us to a hospital in Kenema and treated us free of charge. We were grateful.

We promised the Chief that when we got to Freetown, and when the Lord blessed us, we would not forget about him. Years later, in 1996, on one of our mission trips to Kenema I visited the compound of The Chief at Kasamba Terrace together with some of my ministry colleagues and we reciprocated the kindness shown to us in 1990. I gave them some gifts in the form of cash. Even though they had all forgotten the promise, we remembered the good they had done for us.

We travelled to Bo and stayed at the Seventh Day Adventist (SDA) campus. We were able to stay there because of Clarence's influence since he was a member of the SDA church. He stayed there for one week. Most of these guys wanted to go to Freetown and they did not like Bo. So one day while John went on the soccer field to play, a pastor watched the practice. He admired how John played and his ability to score goals very fast and his control of the soccer ball. He asked John after the game where he came from and John told him that he was a refugee from Liberia and he was with his brother and some friends. The pastor told him that we could visit him whenever we had the chance, and he gave John directions to his house.

The next day we visited the pastor who expressed interest in John. We found out that he was Rev. Samuel Banyinga, the founder and pastor of the Harvest Time Ministry. He was one of the oldest Pentecostal pastors in Sierra Leone.

He gave us food to eat and we had a long conversation about the war and other topics, especially about soccer. He asked us about our plans. Oliver told him that we wanted to go to Freetown but we did not have the money. Pastor Banyinga promised us that he would pay our transport to go to Freetown and that whenever we were ready he should be informed.

The following week we went to Pastor Banyinga and told him that we were ready to travel to Freetown. He gave us the transport and also gave us enough buy food for our journey.

We arrived in Freetown, the capital city of Sierra Leone, on August 15, 1990. We slept in the government broadcasting house which is now the National Headquarters of the Sierra Leone People's Party (SLPP). The next day, we went to Liverpool Street to register with the Red Cross to trace any of our family members with the hope of being reunited.

For months we heard nothing about our family members. However, we received monthly rations from the Red Cross, such as wheat, vegetable oil, canned food, and corn flour. Most of the time, we sold some of our rations to get pocket money to be able to buy rice and cook.

The guys with us did not want to go to the refugee camp at Waterloo, where there were over 20,000 refugees. I suggested that we look for a family that provided lodging for me when I traveled to Freetown in 1988 to visit Fouray Bay College. That trip had been my first time traveling out of Liberia and was a university students' trip. During that trip to Freetown in 1988, we stayed with a Ghanian woman named Mercy.

With some effort, we were able to find Mercy. She was with the Council of Churches in Sierra Leone. We were thankful for her willingness to allow us to stay with her family. When the family first took us in, the lady's husband had travelled to The Gambia to teach. We stayed with her and her children. We brought our ration and gave it to her to cook for all of us. They were very good to us during our stay there. When our ration began to increase, however, and the five of us were getting more food they become jealous and envious. The landlord who lived on the second floor of the house we were staying in began to put pressure on our host. The landlord said that he would increase the rent because he claimed "the Liberian refugees have money" and the food that we were receiving was to him a clear indication. Our host started pressuring us to find another place to live. We told her we did not know anyone and we did not want to go to the refugee camp at Waterloo.

Going to Waterloo meant that we would live in a tent far from Freetown. After increasing pressure, we finally left the house. That night we went to a place called St. John, a major road leading to the western part of Freetown and sat down on the sidewalk. It was almost twelve midnight. We sat there until a Fula man by the name Mr. Bah came near us and asked us what we were doing on the street at that very late hour. We told him that we were refugees from Liberia, and he told us that we should come to stay with him.

We were afraid because we did not know this man and we were processing the offer in our minds. All of us were suspicious that if we went with him something bad might happen. We also encouraged ourselves that because there we were five of us we could possibly defend ourselves in the event of an attack. So we finally decided to go. He took us to a place on 49 Berwick Street. Later on the next day, Oliver, Clarence and Abraham were moved to another house on Victoria Street.

John and I lived with Mr. Bah and his son Salieu in Freetown. His wife and other children were in Guinea. This man was a tailor and was very hardworking. His tailor shop was on Adeliade Street. He ate with the rest of the men in the compound. There was a big bowl that the food was put into and all the men and boys sat around that and ate. If you were not present you missed your food for the day. So John and I used to time ourselves to make sure we were there for food or else we would go hungry the whole day. Everyone staying in this compound was Fula except for John and me. Some of those in this compound that I remember are: Soihebu, Champ, Binta, Jalloh, Tabu, Ramata, Ishaka, and Tejan.

Those of us who fled from the Liberian war zone, were thankful for the peacefulness we discovered in Sierra Leone, especially in Freetown where things were peaceful and normal. More than 150,000 Liberian ıefugces found new hope in the country. The Sierra Leoneans took good care of the refugees. Not many of us lived in refugee camps; we lived with Sierra Leoneans in their homes. This hospitality required great sacrifice on their part.

By March 1991, however, there were signs that the violence we had escaped might find us in Sierra Leone. Around that time, the Revolutionary United Front (RUF) launched an attack in Kailahun, the eastern part of Sierra Leone. The purpose of the offensive was to overthrow the All People's Congress (APC), led by Joseph S. Momoh. The RUF was headed by Foday S. Sankoh, a former corporal in the Sierra Leone Armed Forces. The RUF gathered support and influence. Slowly and far away from Freetown, the threat of civil war began to grow. The RUF's momentum began to increase as they won many to their side.

In May 1991 my friend, Arthur Weay, who had been a classmate at Bassa Junior High School brought a brochure to me. This brochure promoted a Bible school that was starting in Freetown. I accepted it and read the brochure. I told Arthur that I could not go due to lack of money. Later on, I prayed about the opportunity and visited the campus. The next week I told the pastor of the church I was attending of my interest. The pastor, Rev. Nathaniel Dixon of the Robert Street Baptist Church, helped many refugees to stay on the church campus. He told me that he was going to get back with me. Later, he told me that the church would sponsor me to attend the Freetown Bible Training Center. This new turn of events was the beginning of the gradual unfolding of the commitment that I made to the Lord. The unfolding of His purpose became clearer step by step as I sought to obey God.

When I started attending the Freetown Bible Training Center, the administrator called upon me to volunteer in the library. I started working in the library in September 1991 and moved to the office of Freetown Bible Training Center on 29 Regent Road, Freetown. I worked there and stayed there, sleeping in the office where I worked during the day.

By the fall of 1991, the RUF had advanced closer to Freetown. They moved from Kailahun to Kona to Makeni. Located only about two hours from Makeni, Freetown was no longer the place of refuge that we had hoped for in that it was vulnerable to the advancing RUF. Fortunately, the Sierra Leone Armed Forces were strong in the capital Freetown, so an immediate threat was not likely. But the RUF's intentions were to take Freetown if at all possible.

In April of 1992, another development occurred that threatened the stability of Freetown. While the RUF continued to engage the Sierra

Leone Armed Forces, some junior officers of the Sierra Leone Army came to Freetown and overthrew the president of the All People's Congress party, Joseph Saidu Momoh. Those officers represented a faction within the army that believed that Momoh was not equipping them with enough support and weapons to put down the RUF. The overthrow of Momoh was almost a bloodless coup except for a few who were killed trying to defend him. After that coup, the National Provisional Ruling Council (NPRC) assumed authority under the leadership of Captain Valentine Strasser.

One of the changes that occurred soon after the overthrow was the NPRC's declaration of every Saturday as cleaning day. Up until that time, the city of Freetown was extremely dirty. The people thought having the cleaning day was a good decision. We all cooperated and cleaned every Saturday from 6:00 a.m. to noon. The NPRC required all people to help clean, even young children were expected to help.

At that time, Arthur Weay, Lewis Griggs, and I were staying in the FBTC office located at 29 Regent Road, Freetown, on the third floor of the building that the school rented. On cleaning day, NPRC soldiers went from house to house to make sure that everyone cleaned. They also inspected for quality, even the sidewalks in front of compounds. Whoever owned the house or compound was held responsible for its cleanliness. Our responsibility was to clean inside the compound that housed the FBTC office where we stayed. The watchman of the compound was responsible for cleaning the sidewalk outside the compound at its entrance.

One Saturday, the watchman did not clean the sidewalk in front of our compound. He had been drinking heavily the night before and had overslept. My friends and I completed our cleaning that Saturday and then reminded the watchman, who still appeared drunk, that he needed to clean the sidewalk. Then Arthur, Lewis, and I went up to the third floor. We each began to relax. Arthur and Lewis sat in the veranda and talked. I went to the library and began reading my Bible.

When the NPRC soldier inspected our compound, he noticed that the sidewalk had not been cleaned. He asked the watchman to tell him who was responsible for the compound. The watchman told him that the people responsible were upstairs. Then the soldier came upstairs. He saw Arthur first and started beating him with the butt of his gun. I immediately heard Arthur and Lewis yelling. After striking Arthur, the soldier hit Lewis with his gun. Arthur then ran into the library and the soldier followed him. As soon as the soldier saw me, he began hitting me with the butt of his gun. He hit and slightly cut my chest. Then he ordered all of us to go downstairs and clean. Along the way, on all three stories, he continued to slap, kick, and beat us.

Finally, we arrived at the sidewalk and he told us to clean with brooms and shovels. We did so and he continued to yell at us and beat us until we completed the cleaning. Many people came to see what was happening. They watched as we cleaned in embarrassment and endured the abuse. The watchman was nowhere to be seen.

After this incident was finally over, we reported what had happened to the FBTC director. He informed the landlord who then reported the incident to the local commander of that area. They invited us to go to the military barracks to describe the soldier who beat us. We identified him. Nothing was done to the soldier who beat us. Later, however, that soldier came to the FBTC office to apologize to us. We were thankful that our wounds had not been severe enough to be life threatening.

The city of Freetown remained rather peaceful during this period in 1992. Fighting continued to go on between the RUF and the Sierra Leone Armed Forces, but those areas of conflict were far enough away from Freetown not to put us in imminent danger. The government army was able to push back the RUF in certain places, retaking control of Makeni and some parts of Kono. I continued my work at the Freetown Bible Training Center. I did not realize that my life was about to change in a manner that I could never have predicted.

CHAPTER NINE

THE FORBIDDEN MARRIAGE

Little did I know that as a Liberian refugee in Freetown, Sierra Leone, I would meet my wife, Mariama. The circumstances under which we met and developed a relationship are another example of God's grace in my life, especially considering our marriage was forbidden.

Mariama was born into a Muslim tribal group in Africa that is a defender of the Islamic religion, Fulani. Hers was a very strong fundamentalist Islamic group. One day while traveling to the Southern District of Bo, she was in a vehicle accident. As a result of this injury, she was unable to lift a load, bend her back, or carry anything on her back. In Africa, it is essential for a woman to be able to carry things on her back. For many years, she had been unable to do so.

Her parents took her to visit herbalists to perform rituals to heal her back. Those efforts did not work, so they were frustrated and discouraged. After these futile attempts to obtain healing, she heard about an Evangelistic Crusade hosted by Reinhard Bonke to be held at the National Stadium, formerly Siaka Steven Stadium. She decided to attend the crusade.

At the crusade, the Word was preached powerfully. The topic was *everyone was born with a minus/negative but we need a plus/positive*. The plus/positive was depicted as the cross. Following the preaching time, the evangelist gave an altar call for any in the audience who desired a personal relationship with the Lord Jesus. Mariama went forward, prayed the sinner's prayer, and received salvation by faith.

Mariama's salvation experience is an example of application of the following Scriptures:

Romans 10:8-10 (NKJV): [8] But what does it say? "The word is near you, in your mouth and In your heart" (that is, the word of faith which we preach): [9] that if you confess with your mouth the Lord Jesus and believe in your heart that God has raised Him from the dead, you will be saved. [10] For with the heart one believes unto righteousness, and with the mouth confession is made unto salvation.

Romans 10:13 (NKJV): [13] For "whoever calls on the name of the LORD shall be saved."

John 3:14-16 (NKJV): [14] And as Moses lifted up the serpent in the wilderness, even so must the Son of Man be lifted up, [15] that whoever believes in Him should not perish but[a] have eternal life. [16] For God so loved the world that He gave His only begotten Son, that whoever believes in Him should not perish but have everlasting life.

Immediately after Mariama prayed the prayer of salvation, the evangelist said that he would pray for those who were sick. He instructed them to lay their hands on whatever part of their bodies had pain. In faith, she laid her hands on her back. After the prayer, the evangelist said, "Do what you couldn't do before." By faith, Mariama started to bend her back and started jumping up and down. "I am healed; I am healed!" she declared.

Mariama went back home and told her parents about the healing and they rejoiced with her. When she told them that she had become a Christian, however, they were annoyed and then became very angry. They told her to denounce Jesus or she would be killed. Mariama also had three older brothers, two younger sisters, and one younger brother. Her siblings were not supportive of her conversion to Christianity. Fortunately, though, Mariama's brothers and sisters were not in favor of the honor killing that her father advocated. She ran for her life and went into hiding for two years from 1991 to 1993. Many Christians, including Mrs. Adella Masallay, helped her with food, lodging, and clothing during that time.

About two years after Mariama's conversion and life of hiding in and around Freetown, her father and mother moved back to the upcountry near Kenema. They had originally been from the area of Kenema, located near the Liberian border in southeastern Sierra Leone. The family, including

Mariama, fled to Freetown when the RUF rebels advanced from Kailahun toward Kenema. Like many other individuals and families who lived near Kenema at that time, Mariama's family sought the protection of the Sierra Leonean Army near Freetown.

Mariama's parents and some of her siblings moved back to Kenema after the fighting had quieted in that area. When they moved back to Kenema in 1993, that provided some relief for Mariama since she was much farther away from her parents. Subsequent to Mariama's parents' move back to Kenema, fighting between Freetown and Kenema erupted again. That line of conflict isolated Mariama from her parents, and she began to move about more freely in Freetown, relieved of the burden of being found by her parents.

News of Mariama's testimony spread, and I happened to hear about it. I heard, "There is a lady being persecuted because she converted to Christianity." When I heard about Mariama's persecution I became interested in her story. My interest grew even more when I learned that her father wanted to kill her. Mariama's father intended to commit an honor killing, which is taking someone's life because of a conversion to another faith.

My heart was touched by Mariama's pure faith. I was moved. Though I had never seen her, I viewed her as a heroine and wanted to see her. I recalled my own salvation experience and knew that no one had wanted to kill me as a result. I made an arrangement with Sis. Adella Masallay, and she took me to meet Mariama. I went along with another friend, Emmanuel Annan.

When we arrived to meet Mariama, we learned that she was praying. We waited for a very long time before she came to see us. When she came out, we asked her many questions concerning the threat to kill her and how she was living. After some discussion, we prayed with her and left. When I met her I said in my heart to God, "If you give me this woman as my wife, I will be very happy." Yet, I could not tell Mariama what I thought in my heart. I did not see her again until 1993, two years later.

Mariama enrolled as student at the FBTC in 1993. We dated for some time in 1994, growing better acquainted. In February 1995, I proposed for her to marry me. She did not answer me for a very long period. During that time I tried to encourage myself that I could accept a negative answer if she gave one.

As the days passed, I grew more doubtful that she would say yes. In addition to my doubts about her perception of me as a possible husband, I also knew that her parents would strongly forbid the marriage if they knew about it, I continued to meet with her in Bible school, but she never said anything about my proposal! We would meet and talk on campus, but we were not dating like we were when I proposed to her. By May, I had almost lost hope that she would say yes. Then, one day in early June, she stopped by the office with her reply.

She said to me calmly, "Do you remember what you asked me in February?"

Immediately, I was happy that she asked me that question because I knew that I would have a definite answer. Also, because she brought up the topic, hope sprang within me that the answer would be yes.

I said, "Yes, are you talking about the proposal?"

She said, "Yes, I am talking about the proposal." Then she added with a big smile and a twinkle in her eyes, "I have considered what you said, and I am willing to get married to you!"

I felt very happy. I immediately felt like a winner. In Africa, if a man proposes to a woman and she refuses the engagement, that is a shameful defeat to the male. Making a proposal is a very important decision. Anyone with faith in God must pray about that matter seriously before making the proposal. Now that I had my answer, I was excited and relieved and somewhat victorious!

Soon after, we began thinking about the details of our engagement. The expectation was that after the proposal had been accepted a time period of several months at a minimum would be devoted to the engagement period. Cultural traditions demanded that our engagement period would begin when I, as an adult male, brought my parents to meet with the parents of my bride-to-be. That meeting is called the engagement day, but the problem I faced is that my parents were in Liberia and I was in Sierra Leone. Also, Mariama's parents still wanted to kill her as far as we knew and they would certainly not permit the marriage. I prayed about this matter because it represented a new barrier to our relationship.

The alternative that we implemented after praying about it was for me to choose one older couple named David Coomber and his wife to deputize as my parents. Fortunately, Mariama had an uncle who was a police officer in Freetown. He had lived previously in England, so his thinking as a Muslim was different from the mindset of her parents. Whereas her parents were rigid in their views, her uncle—due to his acculturation in England—held a more flexible approach toward religion. He and his wife and Mariama's cousin who was married to an Ivorian Ambassador to Sierra Leone agreed to host the engagement day. They represented Mariama's parents and this event was held at the home of the Ambassador.

After overcoming many barriers, our engagement day was held in October of 1995. We were in the dry season and the summer-like temperatures were quite hot during the day. Engagement day events are held at night. The ceremony involves the groom-to-be arriving with his parents, or in my case deputized parents, and he is not to see the bride-to-be. The groom's party knocks on the door. When the hosts answer the door, the guests are greeted first and then are asked, "For what mission did you come?" With much respect and dignity, the father of the groom-to-be states, "There is a flower in your garden that we came for." Then the parents of the bride-to-be respond that no "flowers" (figuratively) are available. The door is shut and the guests are politely dismissed. At that point, the party of the groom knocks again at the door and is once again greeted and questioned regarding their mission. The exchange is repeated several times until finally, the guests are invited inside.

Once welcomed inside and provided with a place to sit in the immaculately cleaned guest home, the hosts proceed with the communication ritual. During this time, it must be noted, the home is exquisitely decorated with flowers, balloons, streamers, and any other delicate and fitting nicety. In addition, friends and family members are also present in the host's home to witness the ceremony and to participate in it later, after the flower has been selected. The groom is also usually dressed in traditional African attire—for men a full length elegant embroidered gown and a cap. Once comfortably positioned, the host father then asks once again regarding the nature of the mission. Finally, a different answer is provided by the hosts in reply: "Well, it is a good thing that you came to our house this evening. We will bring the flowers in our garden for you to see."

The somewhat humorous part of the ceremony occurs when the parents of the bride-to-be bring in the "flowers" one by one; those flowers are not the flowers that grow in that garden. They have been imported from neighboring gardens (figuratively) for the purposes of this tradition. The father of the groom-to-be knows that this will happen but nevertheless seems a bit surprised to see five to six different females presented to him, one by one, most of whom he has never seen before. As this sequence progresses, the father of the groom-to-be quickly eyes each flower and informs the host father that he has not presented the flower that is sought.

Finally, the father of the bride-to-be presents to the father of the groom-to-be, the bride flower. She, like the groom-to-be, is usually dressed in traditional African attire—for women a full length embroidered gown that is delicate and elegant with hair tucked neatly under a head covering tied in the back. Then the father of the groom-to-be presents the calabash (the basket of food and money) that is presented as a type of dowry. Next, the hosts state their gratefulness by stating, "We thank you for identifying the flower from our garden that you seek. We know you mean well by presenting the calabash." That symbolizes that the groom-to-be will be a responsible person who is able and willing to take care of the bride and assist her parents as needed.

Following the presentation and acceptance of the calabash, the engagement day ceremony is finalized by prayer offered by visiting pastors, a presentation of the ring from the groom-to-be to the bride-to-be, and an announcement of the date planned for the wedding. Following the announcement of the wedding day, everyone present celebrates by eating and drinking and sharing laughter and goodwill. Our engagement day ceremony remains vivid in my memory as a highlight of peace and festivity during a difficult time of war.

Our wedding day was December 14, 1995, and the marriage was held at the King Memorial United Methodist Church in Freetown. Over 1,000 people attended, many from among the 3,000 students attending the Freetown Bible Training Center. In addition to the Maid of Honor, Mariama had ten bridesmaids; I had a Best Man and ten groomsmen. Most of the women attending the wedding were from Freetown and most of the men were from Liberia. With so much talk of war and so many negative reports about violence in Liberia and Sierra Leone, many people were looking for any reason to celebrate something positive.

Samuel and Mariama celebrating

CHAPTER TEN

MINISTRY BEHIND REBEL LINES

I n the midst of war in Sierra Leone, the Lord opened the doors for me to go to Bible school. I attended missionary training school, worked as an administrator at a Bible school, married a Sierra Leonean in 1995, and did pastoral training. I traveled with a team every week from 1996 to 2004 in the interior of Sierra Leone preaching and teaching the gospel to ministers, church workers, and even to soldiers and rebels.

As the Civil War was going on in Sierra Leone we were travelling every week beyond rebel lines to preach the gospel. We conducted more than four major church leaders' conferences at Bo during the war. Most of these conferences were conducted for five days. I travelled at various times with Francis Williams, Eric Warner, David Jallah, Emeric George, and Brother Mark Stewart from the U.S.

In 1996, we traveled toward the Kenema District. While en route, we reached a place in the Bo District called Gerihun. At Gerihum there was a major Kamajor checkpoint. At that checkpoint, all passengers, including the driver, were expected to exit the vehicle and obtain a pass. Then only the driver was permitted to take the vehicle through the checkpoint. The passengers had to walk through the checkpoint and re-enter the vehicle after it had passed.

The problem we faced is that our driver wanted to bribe his way through the checkpoint instead of having us exit the vehicle as the Kamajors expected. This led to confusion between the driver and one of the Kamajors. The Kamajor said that if the driver advanced the vehicle one inch closer to the checkpoint he would shoot the driver and all others in the vehicle. At that point, our vehicle blocked the way of an ECOMOG convoy.

An ECOMOG officer with the convoy approached the Kamajor who held us at gunpoint. I noticed that the stern look of the ECOMOG officer, a very wide and stocky man who held a large gun connected to an ammunition belt that draped across his body. The ECOMOG officer told the Kamajor to clear the way or he would spray him with bullets. When we heard that, we all jumped out of the vehicle, even the driver, and ran off the road into the edge of the bush. The verbal dispute between the ECOMOG officer and the Kamajor followed. Their heated discussion lasted for hours. Finally, another ECOMOG officer resolved the situation and we were allowed to pass.

Some of the other places we travelled for conferences included Bonthe (Mogbwemo), Mattru, Jong, Gbangbatoke, Kono, Kambia, Kukuna, and Makeni. We were in Port Loko in May 1997 from the 20th to 23rd. In Port Loko we conducted a ministers' conference. Unfortunately, the rebels had advanced toward Port Loko and we could hear heavy firing from a close distance. We prayed and asked the Lord to stop the rebels from advancing so the conference could continue. The Lord answered our prayers and we completed the conference while the rebels and the ECOMOG and troops loyal to the government continued fighting.

In May 1997, while we were in Kingtom, we learned that some soldiers had broken away from the Sierra Leone Army. The soldiers entered the city of Freetown early one Sunday in an effort to overthrow Sierra Leone's president, Ahmed Tejan Kabbah. At that time, my wife was pregnant with our first child, Manasseh. The area where we lived was under constant attack. President Kabbah fled to Conakry, the capital city of Guinea. Of course, the overthrow led to much uncertainty. One day soldiers came to our place to search for government supporters. We introduced ourselves as missionaries, and they left quietly without troubling us. Thankfully, the Lord spared our lives.

As the due date for our first child neared, major battles erupted between the Junta and ECOMOG. When the time came for Manasseh's birth in June 1997, we needed to reach the hospital. Unfortunately, the hospital was located about three miles from where we stayed at the time. The route to the hospital required passing through combat zones. We crawled along the way slowly and carefully to finally reach the hospital. Though we were not targeted, sounds of gunfire filled our ears during our cautious journey to the hospital.

After we arrived at the hospital, the doctor said that due to the stress she was under, partly from having to crawl to the hospital, she would not deliver naturally. He said that he needed to perform a C-section. Unfortunately, there was no electricity at the hospital. The transformers and the power lines had been destroyed during fighting.

There was no alternative but to pray. My nephew, Joshua, was there with us at the hospital by that time. We had arrived at about 10:00 a.m., and Joshua arrived at about noon. He and I prayed. Mariama was in the delivery room, where we were not allowed. We sat in a corner of the reception area and prayed. We knew that the only option was for her to deliver naturally. All we knew was that she was in pain and could not deliver.

We prayed and waited all afternoon. Finally, at about 6:00 p.m. on June 3, 1997, one of the nurses came into the waiting area and called us. She said to me, "Your wife has delivered a baby boy safely. Congratulations!"

The nurse escorted me to the large glass window of the room where the newborns were kept. By the natural light that entered from the outside windows, I saw my firstborn son, Manasseh. His name means "God has made me forget my affliction." I felt great and thanked God for his mercy. Due to fighting in the vicinity of the hospital, we could not celebrate with others and that left me with an extreme feeling of loneliness. In our culture celebrating the birth of a child with extended family is highly important, but that would have been impossible at the time.

About one week after the birth of Manasseh, we moved to Spur Road. Because many Lebanese and foreign nationals resided in the Spur Road area, it was a target. Every night the rebels came to loot homes and sometimes killed residents. Girls and women were often raped in that area. Since we had a young child, we prayed and asked the Lord what to do. We had already lived through the war all those years and did not know what to do next. We knew that leaving the area could be perilous. Others who had left due to fear realized their leaving was worse than staying. Some who had left hurriedly by boat drowned because the boat (Pampam as they were commonly referred to in Krio) sank. Others who had departed in vehicles were involved in fatal accidents trying to escape ambushes set by rebels.

We prayed and asked the Lord for guidance. We wanted to know whether to remain in the Spur Road area. If not, we asked the Lord to open another door so that we could leave. Later on that month, we had our answer—and our opportunity. We were in contact with a Fula man who served as a driver for a European ambassador stationed in Freetown.

That driver agreed to take us to a park where we could board a bus that would be travelling on the road to Guinea.

That bus was the only means of transportation that we knew about and had the possibility of boarding. Our interest in this risky plan grew the more we thought about it. We later got on a bus that took us to the Guinean border. Eventually, we safely arrived in Guinea with our young Manasseh. After were had been in Guinea only a few weeks, we received some interesting though disturbing news. The rebels had moved in and taken over the house were we lived on Spur Road. Those soldiers had taken nearly all we left behind and had vandalized the house. We praised the Lord and were reminded of the need to seek God's guidance and to be sensitive to His leading.

In Guinea we stayed with Rev. Siafa Gataweh, who went on to become a missionary to Europe. We stayed at the mission house but things were very difficult. Obtaining food was a struggle. One day I sold a Walkman headset and radio that I had in order to get food for our family. There was food at home but it was not enough due to the needs of other refugees who escaped the war and were staying at the mission house. After about three months of difficulty, a friend who had also fled to Guinea as a refugee approached me. He told me that the director of World Vision of Sierra Leone, Tim Andrews, was looking for us.

After making some preparations the following week, I set out to find the World Vision office at Donka, in downtown Conakry (Enville). I hoped to find Tim Andrews, thinking he could assist us in our dire situation. Rain poured heavily on the day of my trip. Finally, I found the office and the Andrews' dwelling place.

Tim Andrews was happy to see me. We talked about the war in Sierra Leone and about people that we knew and what was happening to them. Before I left his office, the World Vision Director gave me some money to help with food for my family. Mr. Andrews also asked me to come to the office to do some work. I eagerly agreed and began working at the World Vision office as much as I could.

During the time that I worked at the World Vision office in Guinea, I learned to use a computer and to do financial reports in Microsoft Excel. I am very grateful to Angel Roma who was the administrator and finance officer. She was very helpful in teaching me and trained me in many areas of administration. I helped to take care of the petty cash at the office and worked along with a Guinean to do most of the day-to-day work or logistics.

While in Guinea we also spent time with friends to improve our French language skills. Later on during that year, some of our former staff from Sierra Leone came to Guinea. Through the Spiritual Transformation Ministry, we started conducting conferences, training sessions, and crusades in all the refugee camps in Guinea. These ministry efforts took us from east, west, north and south of Guinea. We visited many cities and towns providing conferences and crusades.

We held one of our first crusades and conferences at Camp Dakagbe near the border of Sierra Leone and Guinea. Several people professed salvation through Jesus Christ during this crusade. The local church leaders were encouraged and strengthened during this time of gospel ministry based on God's word. During the crusade some experienced healings and other miracles. Most of those who were healed were Guineans.

Other crusades and church leaders' conferences were held in the various camps, including Musayah Moola, Layah, Farmoria, Kalieh, Gekedou, and Nzerekole. Some of those on the team were Eric Warner (who later went to Norway), David Jallah (who later went to the USA), and Rev. Ade Beckley of Liberty Christian Church in the Lumley area. During those meetings we were privileged to see God heal the blind, the lame, the barren, and the sick. We praise God for His mighty move upon the people who greatly needed His intervention.

In February 1998, we thought that we would be able to leave Guinea to return to Freetown, Sierra Leone. We had been in Guinea for nine months due to the shutdown of nearly all activities in Freetown resulting from the Junta collaborating with the RUF to overthrow Ahmed Tejan Kabba. We still had concerns about security in Freetown. A team of four of us, including Mark Stewart, missionary from the U.S., went to Freetown to stay about a week to assess the situation.

The city of Freetown was almost empty, and only a few people populated the streets. We saw many burned vehicles and buildings as well as a number of burial sites for those who had been killed. The fighting had ended and was under the control of ECOMOG and the army loyal to the government. We decided that we should move back from Guinea after assessing the situation.

Along with several families, we left Guinea in March 1998 and returned to the place we previously stayed at Spur Road. That place had been looted and vandalized by the rebels. Had we stayed there instead of going to Guinea, we probably would have been killed. I thank God for opening up the opportunity to flee to Guinea.

In 1998, after we had arrived back in Freetown from Guinea, we started conducting minister's conferences. David Jalla, Eric Werner, and I planned and led several minister's conferences. Those events were held in places that had been cut off previously due to fighting. Due to the isolation they had experienced while the fighting raged, people in those areas greatly needed spiritual encouragement and revival.

As we knew from experience, traveling to those conference locations involved much risk due to instability and the constant threat of ambush. Eric Warner, David Jallah, and I wanted to hold a conference in Kenema City, located in the Kenema District about 190 miles from Freetown. We had been to that area in 1996 and had an opportunity to return.

After travelling toward the Kenema District for nearly an entire day, we encountered a Kamajor militia checkpoint. The Kamajors told us that they were not going to allow us to cross the checkpoint. Three of them detained us. Because of our Liberian accents, they thought we were Liberian rebels. The Kamajors planned to take us to Kenema City (our destination) for someone to identify us. If no one could identify us, they said they would kill us.

While we prayed silently, an ECOMOG officer stationed at that checkpoint arrived to inquire about the situation. The ECOMOG officer asked, "What is the issue?" He directed his question to us, so we told him while the Kamajor listened silently. The ECOMOG officer then searched our luggage and saw green Gideons New Testaments in all our pieces of luggage. He said the presence of the Bibles indicated that we were not rebels but men of God. He stood for us to be released. That statement led to an argument between the ECOMOG officer and the Kamajor. Eventually, though, we were allowed to pass the checkpoint.

This incident represented yet another intervention of the Lord. We realized that more fully after we reached Kenema City. There we learned that the pastor who was our contact person in Kenema City had travelled to Moyamba. Had the Kamajors accompanied us and sought him to verify our identity, he would not have been present to identity us.

In the absence of our contact, we were hosted by other individuals who knew the pastor who had travelled to Moyamba. We explained to them what happened at the checkpoint. Someone from among their group began to show us knives and other weapons. They said to us, "Let them come, we are ready for them." We were concerned and somewhat confused by those statements. Later, we met with one of the pastors who knew us. He welcomed us and gave us some food. Then he explained to us that they had been expecting a rebel attack in the area and that everyone was tense. They were on edge and suspicious, ready to fight back if necessary. I praised God that the Kamajors did not accompany us; otherwise, the situation might have escalated even though we were innocent servants attempting to minister through the conference.

After six months at Spur Road my wife and I moved to a community called Babadorie. There we rented a basement of a house near a stream. Things were quiet for some time and people started putting their lives back together. We joined most others in thinking and hoping that the war was over. During this period, my wife shared exciting news with me: she was expecting our second child.

I continued to travel as part of a ministry team in the interior of the country and conducted conferences for church leaders and held mass crusades. That time period represented increased hopefulness among the citizens of Sierra Leone. The period of relative calm continued until December 1998.

In December 1998, RUF rebels began to advance toward Freetown. They slowed down because of the Christmas holidays but then began to advance. New Year's Day celebrations were peaceful and the city of Freetown seemed to enter a period of relaxed tranquility. Then violence erupted again on January 6, 1999. Surprisingly, the RUF and AFRC had regrouped. The rebels launched a fresh attack in another effort to take over Sierra Leone. The rebels' code name for this offensive was "Operation Spare no Living Thing."

The time for Mariama to deliver our second child grew nearer. After the rebels had entered the city in January, a curfew was immediately imposed. No one could go outside between the hours of 3:00 p.m. and 8:00 a.m. As a result, Mariama could not visit the doctor regularly. Also, there was a shortage of commercial vehicles for transportation due to the fighting.

In March 1999, Mariama's due date arrived. On March 8, at about 11:00 p.m., she began experiencing contractions. She told me that she was ready to deliver and wanted us to go to the hospital. I immediately thought about the curfew and those who had lost their lives for breaking it. Confusion and tension set in for me as I weighed my options. I felt that my manhood was severely tested at this point. I wondered whether to bravely break the curfew and try to get my wife to the hospital or take a different approach.

After thinking and praying about this situation against the backdrop of my wife's increasing contractions, I made a decision. I called an older woman who lived near us. We asked if she knew a midwife in the area.

That older woman contacted a local midwife to ask if Mariama could deliver where she stayed.

The midwife agreed to help Mariama, but the problem of the curfew remained as a barrier to our leaving the house. I knew that I could not go outside safely. Anytime the soldiers from either faction discovered a male violating curfew, the soldiers shot and killed the male regardless of the circumstances. In some cases, especially with a pregnant woman, there was the hope of mercy being extended. The midwife sent two women that night to help carry Mariama to her place.

Mariama and the women safely reached the home of the midwife. Mariama stayed there during the night but did not deliver the baby. The next morning, after the curfew time ended, I joined Mariama at the home of the midwife. I was then able to go to the hospital with Mariama and the other women who worked with the midwife. On March 9, 1999, Mariama delivered Rebekah at Brookfield Community Hospital, the same hospital where Manasseh was born. We call her Rebekah, but her name is Ephraimnelle, which means "God has made us to be fruitful in a strange land."

Following the birth of Rebekah, we endured about one more month of intense fighting. The violence that began in January 1999 in the Freetown area lasted about four months and subsided in April 1999.

The four months of violence in Freetown changed the city dramatically. Many people were killed. Houses, cars, and buildings were burned and their charred remains were left as reminders of the fighting. Everything in the capital city of Freetown and across the country came to a standstill. There was no work, no school, and no recreation. During this stressful period of violence, we seemed never to have enough to eat. By April 1999, we looked like skeletons.

During that period of intense violence the Lord spared my life many times. All over the city there were checkpoints. One day as I walked toward town after about three months of going nowhere, ECOMOG soldiers stopped me at one of the checkpoints. Immediately, they asked me to identify myself. I showed my identification card to him and from my last name he knew that I was not a Sierra Leonean.

"Are you a Liberian?" asked the officer.

I stood quietly and thought about my response for a long time before replying, "Yes."

At that time, Charles Taylor was accused of sending fighters to help the RUF, so any Liberian was suspect, a potential rebel. By the grace of God, I told the truth. The officer responded, "If you were going to lie, it would have been dangerous for you, but you told the truth and you do not look like one of them." So, he allowed me to pass the checkpoint.

As I passed through the checkpoint, I became tense and fearful, remembering what happened to me in Liberia while travelling from Monrovia to Klay Junction. Secretly in my heart, I began thanking the Lord for His grace, saving me again.

Over time, the rebels assumed control of nearly all of the country and most of Freetown. The ECOMOG forces and the Sierra Leone army managed to defend about half of the western area from the Congo Cross bridge to the peninsula. The rebels captured the eastern, central, and southern parts of the country. In addition, about half of the western parts of Freetown fell.

Initially, few ECOMOG soldiers were available and the Sierra Leone armed forces found themselves outnumbered by tens of thousands of well-armed rebels. Some Liberians joined the rebel forces and fought alongside them. Many Liberians were killed in Sierra Leone as a result of their involvement. Finally, by April 1999, ECOMOG and new re-enforcements pushed the RUF and AFRC to the place commonly known as Okra Hill. Okra Hill is located about 38 miles from the capital city of Freetown.

During those years of war, the Lord afforded us the opportunity to travel through ambushes and war zones to preach and teach the Word. Through this, we saw God's hand upon our lives and ministry. Many lives were transformed; many were saved and healed. Later, we had an opportunity to travel to the Central African Republic (CAR) to provide training. Ironically, we found ourselves once again in the midst of conflict.

Our purpose for traveling to the Central African Republic (CAR) in May 2001 was to train missionaries. Most of those missionaries planned to travel to the Southern Sudan to preach and teach the gospel. We stayed for one week to do the training. The second week, former Head of State Andrea Kpalangba invaded the country from the Democratic Republic of Congo (formerly Zaire). The purpose of the invasion was to overthrow the government of Felix Patisse.

Our lodging was very close to the presidential palace. For three weeks, we stayed indoors while the fighting was going on between the government forces and the rebels. Unless we stayed indoors, we risked being hit by bullets. Even in inside, we kept close to the floor as much as possible and slept on the floor.

The Libyan leader at that time sent military help to fight alongside with the CAR army. The reinforcements helped push back the rebels.

Even though the rebels were pushed back, many people were killed and many buildings were destroyed.

During our stay in the combat zone in CAR, I also had the unfortunate challenge of contracting malaria and not having any medication. Our hosts gave me Amoquine, which is a malaria medication. This pill usually will deplete blood supply and requires additional eating to building up the blood supply. I did not know the side effects of Amoquine. Because the pills were bitter, I took them with sugar. The pills affected my blood, caused me not to sleep well, and made it difficult for me to breathe.

I prayed and read my Bible and trusted the Lord for my healing. This period stands out as a time when I experienced strong attacks spiritually. For almost two weeks I could not sleep at all. Day and night my eyes were open even though I was greatly fatigued.

While we remained in CAR and the fighting continued, the rebels and soldiers alike came into the community to arrest people and kill them. Thankfully, the Lord protected us. No one came to our house. We did not have food to eat for some time, but were happy to be alive.

The CAR government finally defeated the rebels. The destruction had been extensive, and many lost their lives. We resumed our training of missionaries. Even though evil brought on war, the Lord allowed our training to go on successfully despite the delays. One month later, we were free to go. Because of the war and the time that had passed, we had to rebook our flight to Freetown. After that month, we were able to leave CAR safely and return to Sierra Leone.

After I returned to Sierra Leone I saw a doctor as soon as possible. I explained the symptoms I had experienced in CAR, and described the medication I took and its effects. The doctor informed me that I was allergic to Amoquine and proceeded to help me flush the remnants of it from my system.

I recognize that I was not spared or delivered from the various conflicts because I earned that privilege. No one is perfect. I realize that God's grace saved me to enable me to tell of His interventions and the times of my life when he delivered me from danger behind enemy lines.

CHAPTER ELEVEN

TRIUMPH AMID TRAGEDY

The negative aspects of wars in Liberia and Sierra Leone affected all those who lived through the brutal and inhumane conflicts. Despite those dark days, I can look back and see some positive developments that occurred in the midst of the horrible violence. Those blessings—in particular spiritual developments—are a reminder of how the shadow of tragedy cannot completely cover the light of triumph.

One of the first war-related personal tragedies I endured occurred when the University of Liberia closed down on June 4, 1990. That turn of events seemed to unfairly rip from me the opportunity to pursue my plan of completing a pre-med curriculum and enrolling in medical college. Fleeing from Monrovia to Freetown separated me from my dream of attending the University of Liberia. That deep disappointment seemed tragic at the time, but it was only tragic in terms of opportunity cost. Many others lost *all* opportunities as a result of dying in the violence. I am thankful to have survived.

Leaving my home city of Monrovia—where my family had lived for most of my life—was not easy. The violence that surrounded us in July 1990, however, made that decision imperative even though it meant separation from my family. I was fortunate to have reached Freetown, Sierra Leone, by August of 1990. Little did I know at that time that the barbaric violence in Liberia would follow me to Sierra Leone and become perhaps more gruesome there.

Fortunately, soon after arriving in Freetown in August 1990 I had the opportunity to attend the Freetown Bible Training Center (FBTC). That training center was established by Living Water Teaching ministries, which became Living Word Missions. The late Rev. Russell Tatro trained us. Robert Street Baptist church generously paid the fees for me to attend FBTC for two years.

In 1991, I started working with the FBTC. I began as a volunteer, and subsequently was promoted to Library Administrative Assistant. Over time I received a promotion to Assistant Administrator and ultimately to Administrator. At FBTC, I was trained to preach, teach and work in the ministry of helps.

Near the completion of two years of training at FBTC, I began serving at Robert Street Baptist Church as one of the ministers. In addition, I held a few other minor responsibilities with the church. While serving at Robert Street Baptist Church, I completed my ministry studies with a certificate and a diploma. I enjoyed my role at Robert Street Baptist Church and was pleased to serve the body that supported me financially while attending the FBTC as a student. The Robert Street Baptist Church, like all other churches at that time in Sierra Leone and Liberia, faced massive needs among people affected directly and indirectly by war.

After serving at Robert Street Baptist Church for some time, I moved to Glory Ministries to assist the late Rev. Sydney Davies. In 1993, I joined Bethel World Outreach Ministries International when Rev. S. Musa Korfeh and family came to Freetown to start the work there. I served in this church as a Sunday School teacher and was active in the Men's Fellowship. In 1994, I was appointed as one of the ministers of the Bethel World Outreach Ministries, Sierra Leone district. After serving faithfully, I was appointed head of the Covenant Partners and chairman of the Mission Committee.

During those years, I had also continued to work with the FBTC. By that time I held a position as an administrator. Things went well until March of 1996, just after I was married. Leadership discrepancies and inconsistencies began to emerge. I increasingly felt uncomfortable in my position and felt that the director viewed me as a threat since I served as administrator. He knew that I would take a stand if necessary based on what was right.

The director of FBTC pushed hard to have me removed from my position. The FBTC was affiliated with Living Word Missions, based in Tulsa, OK. Staff from the headquarters of the organization told the Sierra Leonean director that I had done nothing wrong. Despite their intervention, I knew that I needed to leave that position. The international board softened that transition by making provision for me to attend the Living

Word Missions School. They also offered for me and my wife to serve in the country of our choice following completion of the school.

Taking a stand in my role as an administrator at FBTC ultimately led to my dismissal from the institution. Staff from the parent organization, Living Word Missions based in Tulsa, OK, thought that I had done nothing wrong. Fortunately, the Living Word Missions organization agreed to investigate the situation further.

At the time in 1996 when I lost my job as an administrator at FBTC, I had no salary or income. My wife and I refused to beg. Unfortunately, some people we had befriended suddenly avoided us. When they saw us, they wouldn't speak to us. Some days we went to sleep, without having eaten that day. We prayed over water, drank it, and went to bed.

Thankfully, God changed our situation through the help of others. People began to bless us. They sent food and money and items to fill our domestic needs. Some of the people who provided support included Pastor Godwin Okoro, Emmanuel Anarobi, Samuel Ironside Williams, Felix Monae, Alfred Weller, Paul Asare, Superintendent M. Jalloh, O.C. Wilson, Nellie Showers, Pastor Emeric Webber, Pastor Joe Oppon, Mr. Sawyer, Pastor Dick Bartholomew, Pastor Eric Warner, Marion Williams, Andy Kennedy, Alfreda Johnson, Mrs. Harvey, Okoro-Cole, Magdalene Menyongar, Brother Russ Tabo, William T. Pastor A. Sam-jolly, Victoria Yemsie-Taylor, Baimba Kabba, Dr. Fofana, and Mark Stewart.

Another turning point occurred as the Living Word Missions organization staff completed their investigation. They discovered that I had sought to protect the image of FBTC. As a result, and to help compensate for what had happened, they offered my wife and me the opportunity to attend the Missionary Training School offered through Living Word Missions. In addition, they offered to allow us to serve in the country of our choice after completing the missionary training school.

Later, in 1996, my wife and I accepted our scholarships from Living Word Missions and attended their missionary training school. Our involvement at the missionary training school included three months in class followed by practical application. We travelled around to various villages in Sierra Leone and visited other countries to apply what was learned in the classrooms of the Living Word Missionary Training School. Next, we attended more classes and followed that with more travel and practical application of what we learned. Ultimately, we both obtained a certificate in missions.

At the Living Word Missionary Training School, we met and interacted with individuals from various countries, including Ghana, Nigeria,

Cameroon, the U.S., Liberia, and Sierra Leone. My wife and I went on several missionary trips and those trips helped us to be the people we are today. Traveling with Mariama under the duress of war brought us much closer together, and we grew mutually in our relationship with God. Though neither of us could have ever predicted that we would serve in a missionary capacity, we began to realize that God was orchestrating our lives for His purposes.

One of the students from the U.S. who attended the Living Word Missionary Training School was Mark T. Stewart. He traveled to the school from his home in Anderson, SC. I enjoyed meeting Mark and discussing missionary opportunities with him. After we completed our training, Mark and I started working together in missions work in addition to some other activities that I was engaged in during that time.

Samuel and Mark Stewart at Konde Farm

Mark Stewart and I traveled around the country of Sierra Leone during the years of war. Most of the missionaries had left the country due to the conflict and violence. Mark and I conducted interdenominational pastors' conferences. The Lord protected Mark and me many times. We survived a number of possible ambushes and happened upon multiple ambushes just after they had occurred. On several occasions, the Lord protected us as we gained access through difficult checkpoints. I learned much during that time of service as we worked with church leaders. Mark and I continued to develop in practice the leadership skills we had studied during the missionary training school.

Mark Stewart and I worked together in Sierra Leone until 1999. At that time, Mark moved to Kenya to be able to minister to Somalians. He emphasized training those ministers to return to their various churches for evangelistic service. The decision to move to Kenya was very difficult for Mark. He felt God leading him in that direction, so he obediently went even though the transition included a number of challenges. Mark served in Kenya for several years. Later, he moved back to the U.S. with his family. While living in the U.S. with his wife and daughter, Mark continued to travel periodically to Africa and other parts of the world. I always enjoyed seeing him whenever possible.

While serving with Mark Stewart in various missions work, I also experienced some other interesting ministry developments. In 1997 I was invited to work with the International Missionary Center (IMC) in the early stages of the ministry. We traveled around the country to about ten districts, to cities, towns and villages, preaching, teaching and planting cell churches. Those responsibilities took me to Ghana, Ivory Coast, Guinea, The Gambia, Ghana, Central Africa and South Africa. These trips exposed me to international ministry where I established relationships with many ministries around the world.

In January 1998, leaders within Bethel World Outreach Ministries recommended me to be licensed as a minister. That ceremony took place in Abidjan, Ivory Coast. In 2002, Bethel World Outreach Ministries recommended me for ordination. That ceremony took place in Bumjuburum, Ghana. Bishop Dr. Darlingston G. Johnson, General Overseer of Bethel World Outreach Ministries International conducted the licensure and ordination ceremonies.

One of the greatest things that happened during the war in Sierra Leone was the visit of Brother John Robb and his team to Freetown. In conjunction with the International Prayer Council, they hosted a Prayer Summit for 1500 pastors and prayer leaders from May 2–4, 2000. The theme of the Prayer Summit was from 2 Chronicles 7:14, which states, "If My people who are called by My name will humble themselves, and pray and seek My face, and turn from their wicked ways, then I will hear from heaven, and will forgive their sin and heal their land."

The team of intercessors gathered for the Prayer Summit included representatives from the United States, Germany, Nigeria, Lesotho, and Rwanda. Specific prayers were raised during the three-day prayer summit. People prayed for Sierra Leone to repent of sin and ask God to forgive them of the sins of their forefathers such as cannibalism, ritualistic killings, occultism, and secret societies. People prayed for the Lord to bring the war to an end quickly because of the many deaths and suffering. People prayed for the rebel leaders to be arrested and for those who committed atrocities to be put on trial for war crimes.

The prayers of the many people of faith in Sierra Leone are an example of people coming together with a solemn yet hopeful belief that things could get better by the grace of God. Though it's horrible that such grave circumstances must compel individuals to pray fervently as a group, it's encouraging that faithful prayer is practiced during dire times. The many prayers for the conflicts to end were replaced with prayers for restoration and the rebuilding process.

God answered those prayers. One of the former warlords, Johnny Paul Koroma, who had recently gotten saved attended the Prayer Summit. Koroma asked for the team to pray for him. Then he broadcast a message over the radio. Koroma asked that everyone go outside at 6:00 p.m. and shout the name of Jesus seven times and declare that the war is over. For the first time in Sierra Leone, Christians, Muslims, Hindus, Buddhists, and others came out and in unison shouted the name of *Jesus*. Not long after this dramatic event, the RUF leader, Foday S. Sankoh was arrested and his demoralized group was defeated.

That turn of events reminds me of Psalm 125:1-2: "They that trust in the LORD shall be as mount Zion, which cannot be removed, but abideth forever. As the mountains are round about Jerusalem, so the LORD is round about his people from henceforth even forever." The great spiritual turning point occurred when thousands participated in Johnny Paul Koroma's call to shout the name of Jesus seven times. The prayer conference in May 2000 seems to have been instrumental in turning the spiritual tide in Sierra Leone as well as influencing the war favorably.

Following the arrest of RUF leader Sankoh, the number of UN forces increased in Freetown. The strong presence of UN forces in Freetown enabled the UN to implement the Demobilization, Detraumatization, Rehabilitation and Reintegration (DDRR) program. Any rebel that turned in a weapon got $150.00 for each weapon handed over. Through the DDRR program, the former rebels were then trained in skills such as carpentry, construction, soap making, driving, etc.

In 2001, as the war in Sierra Leone began to lessen in intensity, I enrolled in the Evangelical College of Theology. This institution had been formerly named Sierra Leone Bible College. While attending the Evangelical College of Theology, I worked for the International

Missionary Center based in Freetown. As part of that work, I traveled to the Central African Republic, Ghana, Nigeria, The Gambia, Guinea, Burkina Faso, Ivory Coast, and Niger. My main responsibility was to train others to show *The Jesus Film*. I also helped coach Christian leaders to form cell groups in their homes to begin new churches.

I had traveled to multiple countries in Africa, but I had never left the continent. In 2002, I learned of a special travel opportunity. Leaders from the Gideons International organization invited me to attend their international convention in Louisville, KY. This large convention would include representatives from all over the world. The interesting events that led to my invitation from the Gideons require some explanation.

During the approximate ten years of war, the Gideons International usual means of distributing Bibles and New Testaments had been severely disrupted. As I traveled with our team to many towns and villages behind the lines of fighting, we distributed Gideon's New Testaments. On those trips, we often realized that vehicles in front of us had been recently ambushed on the same roads we traveled. We came across several instances of ambushed vehicles and saw dead bodies and destroyed vehicles. Fortunately, we did not experience an ambush directly.

On one trip, we encountered some rebels from the RUF in partial military uniforms. The rebels were stealing from a vehicle recently ambushed as part of a convoy. Dead bodies lay in multiple ambushed vehicles. We came across this ambush scene quickly before we realized how close we were to the RUF rebels. They were in the process of stealing parts from an engine. Smoke and the smell of burning oil filled the air. I remember the fierce appearance of these rebels. On their faces were black paint and white chalk used to help disguise their identity. About four of them were working on getting parts from the engine; along both sides of the road more stood with guns in hand. Those who saw us looked sharply at us and motioned us to go through quickly. We sped away and they did not harm us. In our vehicle at that time were Mark Stewart, David Jallah, Eric Warner, myself, and the driver.

Leaders from the Gideons organization knew about our distribution of New Testaments in such circumstances. On one occasion, we had given a Bible to one of the chaplains of the Sierra Leonean Army. The chaplain's name is Moses Kargbo. He had accepted a Gideons New Testament and placed it in his front shirt pocket. In addition to his role as chaplain, he served in the infantry and participated in combat. During an exchange of gunfire he was shot, but the Gideons New Testament in his pocket helped save his life.

Later, Mr. Kargbo shared his testimony with a Gideons representative named Ronald Cummings. Mr. Cummings, a Canadian, served as the Regional Field Officer for Gideons International. One of the countries Mr. Cummings worked with was Sierra Leone. After Mr. Kargbo shared his testimony, Mr. Cummings invited me to attend the Gideons International Convention.

I attended the Gideons International Convention in Louisville, KY, in July 2002. I represented Sierra Leone and shared about our ministry efforts there. I gave a report about the distribution of Scripture in Sierra Leone and described some of the conditions under which we distributed New Testaments. The Gideons wanted to raise awareness of and garner support for the need to distribute Bibles in Sierra Leone as the war came to a close.

Visiting the U.S. for the first time involved much anticipation and excitement. What I saw was unlike anything I had ever seen. The abundance of food and the infrastructure such as roads and bridges were beyond anything I had experienced. After years of war in Sierra Leone and after seeing the condition of various countries in Africa, I enjoyed the safety and the conditions of traveling in the U.S.

After attending the Gideons Conference in Louisville, KY, I had the opportunity to visit Tulsa, OK. In Tulsa, I gave a report to leaders of Victory Christian Center, the organization that had supported crusades and church leader conferences in Freetown and Makeni, Sierra Leone, in 2001. After visiting Tulsa, I went to Anaheim, CA, to report to Campus Crusade for Christ (currently called CRU) leaders about our progress in showing *The Jesus Film* in Africa. I also visited my sister, who at that time lived in Atlanta, GA.

While in the U.S., I called Mark Stewart. When he learned that I was in the U.S., he asked me to come to Anderson, SC. I agreed, and Mark bought my bus ticket to travel from Atlanta to Anderson. We met in Anderson at Mark's father's house. His father has since died. Brother Mark informed me that he was planning to start a new ministry. He wanted me to be involved in the new ministry. Mark explained to me his ideas for the new ministry. That ministry later became known as Hope Universal.

As I reflect on all of the tragedies that occurred during the periods of war in Liberia Sierra Leone, I can't help but think about how God enabled me to intersect with Mark Stewart. I am amazed when I think about my dismissal from FBTC and the opportunity it provided to attend missionary training school. At that the missionary training school, I met Mark Stewart in 1996. Mark and I were able to meet in the U.S. as a result of my invitation to attend the Gideons International Convention in 2002. When I met Mark in Anderson in 2002, I did not realize that such a large part of my future would be linked to Hope Universal.

In 2002, I started serving as one of the leaders of Hope Universal in Sierra Leone. Over time, this organization, under the leadership of Mark Stewart, has been able to build a medical clinic in Sierra Leone, run a Bible school for church leaders, and initiate well water projects. Brother Mark has been very supportive of my family spiritually, financially, materially and morally. Through Hope Universal, we were able to do greater work in the Lord's Kingdom. I have been able to speak to TV and newspaper reporters and present in churches, schools, and business organizations because of Mark T. Stewart. He is a great example to us and many Christians in Africa. He is indeed a missionary who has contributed much to the lives of others and continues to do so.

Partly through my interactions with Hope Universal, I am also thankful to have worked with Mrs. Katja Starkey, a Christian who lives in Omaha, Nebraska. She and her family have been very instrumental in bringing awareness to her city of the atrocities and mayhem committed during the wars in Sierra Leone and Leone. Through her non-profit organization, Touch the Nations, I was able to speak at schools, churches, organizations, and the local university, I also participated in an interview conducted by *The Omaha World Herald*. I shared the story of the tragic wars and the people in the Omaha area responded with concern and support.

Throughout that time period of expanding ministry opportunities, I continued to progress in my academic studies as a student at the Evangelical College of Theology. Though balancing work and travel and family life proved difficult, the grace of God allowed me to complete my degree in less than four years. Some of my college mates were Bindi Thomas, David Sankoh, Paul Conteh, Eric Manso, George Samura, Suliaman Conteh, Samuel Kargbo, Elisabeth Sowa, Georgiana Malige, Agnes Lamin, and Angel Ama-Lamin Thorpe. In 2003, I graduated with honors from the Evangelical College of Theology with a Bachelor of Arts degree in Ministries/Adult Education.

Beginning in October 2003, I accepted leadership of the International Missionary Center or Africa Center for World Missions. Under my leadership, and with the support of my wife and our ministry team, we were able to have umbrella organizations – TTN/COI. We planted seven cell churches and launched a new project to reach students.

I thank God for all those who helped shape my life spiritually and were supportive of increased ministry activity. Special thanks go to Rev. Toby Gbeh, Deacon Kolay Paul, Sister Jessica, Rev. Ralph Lampkins, Donald Osman, Rev. Peter Amos George, Rev. Eddie Gibson, Rev. Ernest T. Lewis, Rev. Musa Korfeh, Rev. Mensah Otabi, Archbishop N. Duncan Williams, the late Rev. Archbishop Ben Idahosa, Rev. Kenneth Hagin, Bishop Thomas D. Jakes, Rev. Myles Munroe, Rev. Julius K. Laggah, Bishop Darlingston G. Johnson, Rev. Evg. Lawrence Kennedy, Rev. Russ Tatro, David Orr, Evg. Bert Farias, my parents Deacon and Mrs. Samuel Dee Menyongar, Sr., Mark T. Stewart, Larry Reeves, Kent McGahey, Joe Bacher, John Maxwell and Ben Carson. Brother Keith and Sister Laura Padgett have been great encouragement and support to us through the Change One International Ministries. With their support we have been able to minister to many in Sierra Leone.

Despite the ravages of war that engulfed my homeland, followed me into Sierra Leone, and threatened my future, the Lord has enabled me to experience triumph in the midst of tragedy. I have had the privilege of serving in a ministry role in Liberia, Sierra Leone, Guinea, Ivory Coast, The Gambia, Ghana, Nigeria, Mali, Burkina Faso, Niger, Central African Republic, South Africa, Europe and the United States. The Lord has opened doors for me to speak at large and small crusades; at conferences for pastors, church workers and church leaders; at outreaches for amputees, war wounded, orphans, policemen, military personnel, prisoners, students, those in hospitals; at medical outreaches; and at *The Jesus Film* events.

I am what I am today by the grace of God. As long as I have breath I will continue to serve the Lord. Scripture assures me that nothing will separate me from the love of God (Romans 8:35). The Lord taught me that serving Him occurs in times of peace as well as times of conflict. Though I prayed at one time for God to end the war so I could serve Him, I now know that the tragedies of our lives often are the very circumstances in which the Lord enables us to experience triumph—through His strength and not our own.

CHAPTER TWELVE

BEYOND WAR

The Civil War in Sierra Leone began later (1991) and ended earlier (2002) than the two Civil Wars in neighboring Liberia, which ran from 1989 to 1996 and 1999 to 2003 respectively. In 2002, the war in Sierra Leone officially ended. Thousands of arms and ammunitions from rebel forces were burned at Lungi International Airport in a ceremony symbolizing the restoration of peace. By 2003, the conflict in Liberia officially ended. UN peacekeeping troops exerted a strong presence in both countries.

According to reports from the United Nations, approximately 70,000 individuals were killed during the Sierra Leone Civil War (1991-2002). Additionally, an approximate 10,000 more were amputated and over 2.6 million were displaced due to war. The UN also reports that that in Liberia an estimated 250,000 were killed (mostly civilians) and that hundreds of thousands of refugees fled to neighboring countries.

The Lord took us through those wars. Even though it was difficult, we survived by the grace of God. The post-war nations of Sierra Leone and Liberia are continuing their transformation. The church is growing and more people are coming to the Lord. My prayer is that God will provide for both nations leaders who fear Him and love others. Bad things can and will happen, but we have a great God.

I have also prayed for years that those who were involved in the horrible wars in Liberia and Sierra Leone will be able to move forward through reconciliation. The first step is to help people get over the haunting fear and overwhelming guilt by helping them understand that no matter what they have gone through and no matter what they have done, they are still loved by God. Despite the fact that the pain is unbearable, God loves them despite the atrocious things they did; God has not given up on them. That must be the foundation.

Reconciliation is a gradual process that involves repentance. What is repentance? It occurs when an individual who has done wrong recognizes that he or she was wrong and asks God for forgiveness. Repentance is both a mental and spiritual exercise. It involves our turning to God as we realize our need to agree with Him about all matters.

Repentance is followed by restitution. What is restitution? This process involves the perpetrators and the survivors and the perpetrator asking the survivor or victim for forgiveness and the survivor also accepting the forgiveness and returning it to the perpetrator also. In showing genuine restitution, the perpetrator can go beyond and do something by helping the survivor or victim to get back on track in any way possible.

Of course, there are barriers to reconciliation. The lack of courage hinders reconciliation. So too does holding on to hatred. Perhaps ongoing hatred is the greatest barrier, and many people refuse to give up hatred. Unless people deal with the spirit or attitude of hatred, those who hold onto it will allow their hatred to burst forth one day, possibly causing more violence and restarting a vicious cycle. Fear is another barrier. There is fear of change, a natural fear that people experience, especially in relation to forgiving or asking forgiveness. In every community people know others involved with evil, and they often fear retribution.

For a person to forgive breaks the power that hatred holds. The truth is that those who don't forgive slowly die from their lack of forgiveness. The bitterness eats them up. Forgiving restores health and vitality.

Wars, rebellion, floods, drought, famine, earthquakes and pestilences are not good. But out of the evil that happens, God always can make something good. Even as a result of the wars, some good things happened. For example, more people came to the Lord than ever in the history of Liberia and Sierra Leone. Another positive outcome was that many learned how to forgive. Slowly over time many have had their trust and confidence restored. I thank God for His taking something so awful and providing some positive outcomes.

The book, *Faith Under Fire*, was written by a friend, Antoine Rutayisire, who visited Sierra Leone and Liberia and prayed that God would bring the wars to an end. He wrote, "Israel was a Hutu man who lived what he preached . . . and he preached against ethnic hatred." In the 1972/1973 massacres, he protected a Mututsi student who was his school mate by covering him with his own body and taking the beating while his friend escaped the attackers. He joined Tutsi and Hutu Christians to conduct Bible Studies in his home.

While conducting a meeting in February of 1994, a hand grenade was thrown into Brother Isreal's home as a warning. Friends asked him to stop the Bible study. He said, "What Christian testimony would that be? I have been preaching reconciliation, and I will live it, even if I have to pay for it with my own blood." Pay with his blood he did. He was gunned down the very first day of the massacre in April of 1994 along with three daughters. Only one daughter survived.

Brutal examples like the one involving Brother Israel's seem difficult to process. But we find comfort in verses such as Nehemiah 13:2 which refers to evil but states, "Howbeit, our God turned the curse into a blessing." The devil meant all these wars for evil—to destroy and kill. But we read in John 10:10, the Lord Jesus helps us to overcome: "The thief cometh not, but for to steal, and to kill, and to destroy: I am come that they might have life, and that they might have it more abundantly." In the midst of the war, the Lord caused us to be strong. We went through all the trials, but came out victoriously.

When the apostle Paul came to the end of his ministry journey, he said, ". . . the time of my departure is at hand. I have fought the good fight, I have finished the race, I have kept the faith" (2 Timothy 4:6–7). Paul modeled a life of moving forward in faith. He finished well. Do we have the faith and vision to continue to move forward in spite of all obstacles, barriers, trials, difficulties, adversities, discouragement and hindrances?

When we finish our journey or race here on earth, may it be said of each of us, "Here lies a person who faithfully served the Lord, ran well, and finished well." Not only may that be said of us, but may we also hear, "Well done, thou good and faithful servant: thou hast been faithful over a few things, I will make thee ruler over many things: enter thou into the joy of thy lord" (Matthew 25:21). Until then, may we find in the grace of God the power of forgiveness and the possibility of reconciliation.

With the end of the war in Sierra Leone came new opportunities for the country to grow and develop. Similarly, my individual path of development broadened after I graduated from college. The quality of information determines the quality of destiny. As I examine the ups and downs of the sub-region of West Africa, I see the need for greater conflict restoration, healing, reconciliation, peace building and development. As I hope for these positives to occur, I am reminded of Albert Einstein's quote: "We cannot solve our problems with the same thinking we used when we created them."

I knew that my level of knowledge would determine the level at which I could operate. I also knew that my level of knowledge would determine the quality of my destiny. Simply having a vision was not enough. I needed foresight (motivation from looking ahead), insight (how to accomplish the vision), and a strategy for accomplishing my goals. My observations suggest that success depends on how much knowledge I have as well as what I do with it.

As I considered my own need for development, I knew that additional education would carry benefits beyond what I could conceive. With that view of education in mind, I began pursuing a Master of Science degree in Development Studies at Njala University in Sierra Leone. In February 2009, I completed my Master of Science degree at Njala University. I decided to study development because of the wars that have plagued our sub-region in West Africa. Clearly, there is great need for developing and rebuilding the countries in that region.

My dissertation was entitled "Non-Government Organizations and Community Development: A Case Study of the Western Area." I will consider furthering my education as the Lord leads and provides. As Ben Carson stated, "After you have used all that you have learned what helps you to continue to make it is the gift that God has given to you. Your gift will manifest when what you learned tries to give way. "

Continuing with higher education has helped me to mature. My college experiences have affected me like they will anyone: helping me shape my thinking and decision making. For example, when I completed high school I used to think that my country Liberia was the best and most beautiful country in West Africa. When anyone criticized my country I got angry and wanted to fight back. I argued not based on actual facts but based upon patriotism or nationalism. For instance, when Liberia was playing a soccer match against a neighboring country even though I knew that the opposing team was far better than the Liberian Lone Star, I would think one-sided and say everything good concerning our team. I could not see the good side of the other team. As time went on, my thinking matured and I gradually began basing my arguments on balanced facts instead of merely choosing one side.

Through continued education I am better able to think objectively and look at issues from both sides: the positive and the negative. This process of maturity also taught me that in every country there are good and bad people. There are people who love foreigners and those who hate foreigners; therefore, I should not generalize that all the people in a particular country are wicked or promote xenophobia.

One of the tragedies that turned to triumph was the alteration of my educational plans. Reflecting even now on the closing of the University of Liberia in 1990 is painful. However, the wasted years of civil war did not stop me. Those years only delayed me. I suffered and missed lots of opportunities, but my aspiration and zeal were not broken.

Obtaining my bachelor's and master's degrees required a long time, but the goals were achieved. Linked to my education were opportunities for me to travel around Africa, to the USA, and to Europe. During the war, God even provided a wife for me that fears Him, and He has blessed us with beautiful children. War is not a good thing, but God can change the situation of war and turn it for His glory to honor Himself.

My younger brother, John Menyongar, survived the war and experienced success in the years following. I referred to him earlier as Pekin John, the term "Pekin" being used to denote his youth at that time. The events of his life are another example of God's grace.

John Menyongar was born on June 26, 1979. He is the last son of our father. Unlike the rest of Menyongar children, John was born in Monrovia, Liberia, after we moved there from our village near Cesstos. He always walked along with our father since he was the youngest. It seemed that anything John wanted, father was willing to get for him; being the youngest in the family has its privileges all over the world!

As a young child, John showed interest in football (soccer). He loved to watch and to play when he had the opportunity, even at an early age. One day he asked our father for a soccer ball, and his wish was granted. That toy served more as a tool for John given his interest in the sport.

When John entered the Monrovia Demonstration Elementary School on Clay Street he started playing for his school's team. His skills immediately contributed to his team's success. John scored so many goals for his team that Monrovia Demonstration Elementary School won the championship for the National Elementary School League.

That victory caused his friends and classmates to carry him high on their shoulders around the major streets in Monrovia before they carried him home with great fanfare. The Menyongar family overflowed with excitement. I remember our father saying during that celebration that "everything that a Menyongar does usually comes out to be great." Our father did not hide his satisfaction with the great performance of his youngest son.

John also played for his junior high school and senior high school and went on to play for the champion team of Liberia, the Mighty Barrolle. Before and during that time, John helped his team win many trophies.

Just as my college plans were put on hold when war came to Monrovia, John's soccer plans appeared to fade. He and I fled Monrovia to walk to Sierra Leone to escape the war. After we arrived in Sierra Leone, however, opportunities for John to play soccer emerged despite the undesirable circumstances that soon plagued the nation.

While in Sierra Leone, John played for the Port Authority team. In one game played at the national stadium, John amazingly scored five goals. John stayed in Sierra Leone for a few months with me until ECOWAS sent a peacekeeping force to Liberia (ECOMOG) and installed Professor Amos Sawyer as interim leader of the transitional government. At that point, in 1991, John got on a ship and went back to Monrovia, Liberia, where the fighting had been quelled for a period of time.

Back in Liberia, John completed his Senior High School at AME Zion High School in Monrovia. He played soccer for his high school team. After graduating, he played for the Mighty Barrolle football club based in Monrovia. Later, John played for the Lone Star, the Liberian National Team. John played in many national and international matches in and out of Liberia. He served as captain of the Lone Star Team.

Later, John travelled to Hungary to play professional soccer. He stayed there until 1997. Then he came back to Liberia for a while and later moved to the U.S. in 1998. While in the U.S., John (known by his soccer name Johnny) played intercollegiate soccer at Lindsey Wilson College. (On official Liberian rosters, he is listed as John Menyongar.) While at Lindsey Wilson College, John led his team to an NAIA Division III national championship.

John signed his first professional contract in the U.S. in 2000 with the Minnesota Thunder after impressing at a tryout camp. John spent the first six seasons of his professional career with Minnesota, totaling 50 regular-season goals in addition to many playoff and Lamar Hunt U.S. Open Cup tallies. He helped the Thunder to the 2003 A-League championship game and scored five goals as Minnesota reached the semifinals of the 2005 Lamar Hunt U.S. Open Cup.

In November 2005, John signed with the Rochester (New York) Raging Rhinos, where he was chosen as team MVP in 2008 and 2009. Prior to the 2010 season, he became the first signing for the new club NSC Minnesota. John played soccer for the NSC Minnesota Stars in the USSF Division 2 Professional League.

John Menyongar in action

John has played in two qualifying matches for the 2002 FIFA World Cup, and played in two matches at the 2002 African Nations Cup. John played four matches during the team's qualifying campaign for the 2006 FIFA World Cup, but the team lost 0-2 against Senegal. He also captained the team from 2004-2006.

In 2011, John transitioned from the NSC Minnesota team by signing with the United Sikkim Sports Club in India. Since that time, John has continued to excel in soccer and has played for multiple soccer leagues in India, including the Shillong Lajong Football Club and the Dempo Sports Club.

As of 2013, my brother and his wife are expecting their third child to add to the son and daughter they already have. His family live in Fridley, MN. When John is not traveling, he joins his wife and children in attendance at a Baptist Church near their home.

My brother John and I were fortunate to have survived the wars in Liberia and Sierra Leone. The lives of many others of our friends and extended family members were lost during those conflicts. I remember them with respect. I am humbled each time I think about the devastating effects of those wars.

To move beyond war, we must not allow the negative effects of war to dominate our thinking. The many horrors and tragedies cannot be adequately described, nor can the depth of emotion and loss be adequately expressed for those who endured the inhumane violence. Hope is not lost, however. Hope for me is found in the strength of a loving and sovereign God. In my case, I recognize that He saved me spiritually. Yes, He has saved me physically many times, but the most important point is that He has saved me spiritually.

When I reflect on the effects of war, I am often reminded of various Scriptures. One that sometimes comes to mind is Genesis 50:20. In that narrative about Joseph, we see Joseph's ability in God's strength to comment positively on negative events. He stated to the brothers who had betrayed him, "But as for you, ye thought evil against me; but God meant it unto good, to bring to pass, as it is this day, to save much people alive" (KJV). Joseph went from the pit to Potiphar's house; he then went from prison to the palace. Seventeen years passed between his dream and the fulfillment of it. The presence of evil is a reality in life, but the grace of God is sufficient as He works His purposes.

What have I learned from bad things? Many lessons can be gleaned from adversity. A few that come to my mind are that bad things tend to make us believe we have been reduced to nothing. Despite that tendency, I can use the crisis as a stepping stone and overcome it. Every conflict has a solution and every person seems to have his or her own view. But when parties can listen to one another and get involved in a healthy dialogue, then triumph can occur. Keys to that process are trust and confidence in God, both of which are absolutely essential for deliverance.

Adversity became a breeding ground for success for those who strove not to be characterized by the conflict they experienced but by their response to the challenges they faced. Their success required sacrifice, but God strengthened them. II Corinthians 12:9-10 states, "But He said to me, my grace is sufficient for you, for my strength is made perfect in weakness . . . for when I am weak, then I am strong." Those who were fortunate enough to survive and who faced adversity responsibly were able to apply the words of Theodore Roosevelt, the 26th president of the United States. Roosevelt stated, "Do what you can, with what you have, with where you are "

One of the great illustrations that I have been fascinated with is the process for producing table salt. To produce table salt, we need sodium

(Na) and chlorine (Cl). Sodium is a neutral element. Chlorine has three characteristics; it is colorless, odorless, and poisonous. When the sodium is added to the chlorine, it has the capacity to neutralize the poison in the chlorine. The result is table salt, free from poison and good to eat. Just as the sodium neutralizes the poison in the chlorine, the grace of God is *spiritual* sodium that has the ability to neutralize every poison or adversity that we go through. When I am weak, oppressed, depressed, suppressed, discouraged, tormented, fearful or hopeless, the grace of God is sufficient for me . . . and for you.

Adversity is the problem, the trouble, the challenge, the difficulty, the opposition, and the *opportunity* that we face daily. As long as we are in this world, we will face adversity. Such trials were referenced by the Lord Jesus (John 16:33). Some of the adversities that I and many others face around the world, specifically in Africa, are poverty, diseases and war.

By the grace of God I have come through three wars and survived them. In the war's wake, nearly every aspect of life had to be viewed from a pre- and post-war perspective. In my case, the post-war perspective is that God enabled me to survive. Beyond enabling me to survive, God equipped me through the adversity of war for the purpose He has for me to fulfill.

PART II

CHAPTER THIRTEEN

SURVIVE FOR PURPOSE

As a child, my future took a precarious turn one morning in 1973 before I left for school. From atop the old wooden chair I sat in, I fell into a pot of boiling water that my mom planned to use for bathing. Much of my back and legs were badly burned. I spent the next three months in the hospital in much pain recovering from second degree burns. The Lord healed me, but the scars are still on my body.

In spite of the horrible mishap, I survived. Burn scars do not disappear easily. Beyond the physical scars are the memories of negative events that scars often represent. Everyone should actively try to prevent any form of burn on their bodies. Yet, such burns occur all too often. My view of those scars is not altogether negative, however. Each time I see them, I am reminded of my persuasion that God has a purpose for every person born into this world.

Life without purpose is a tragedy and without meaning. Purpose is the reason for existence or the intended reason for our being on earth. God does nothing in life without a purpose. One Scripture that comes to mind is Proverbs 19:21: "There are many plans in a man's heart, nevertheless the LORD's counsel—that will stand." Another Bible verse about purpose is Isaiah 14:24: "The LORD of hosts has sworn, saying, 'Surely, as I have thought, so it shall come to pass, And as I have purposed, so it shall stand.'" How sad it would be for us to stand at death's door having never known the purpose for which God created us.

Everything and everyone in life has a purpose. Ecclesiastes 3:1 states, "To everything there is a season, a time for every purpose under heaven." In Proverbs 15:22, we read, "Without counsel, plans go awry, but in the multitude of counselors they are established." I am completely convinced that the Lord delivered me from the midst of three deadly and vicious civil wars in Liberia, Sierra Leone and the Central African Republic because he has a purpose for my life. His purpose for me is not merely for my benefit, but for the benefit of others.

I survive for the purpose of telling how God can give hope to the hopeless, defense to the defenseless, courage to the discouraged, victory to the victimized, and motivation to the unmotivated.

I survive for the purpose of telling the uncountable horrific ordeal of many unfortunate people who cannot tell it.

I survive for the purpose of showing that God is able to change a mess into a miracle, to transform what man says is impossible into a possibility.

I survive for the purpose of forgiving those who did evil to us, so that by our example, others will be willing to forgive.

I survive for the purpose of glorifying God, who is able to take any person and make him or her a vessel, regardless of the person's past or present situation.

I survive because no one is born as a biological mistake or by accident. There is an answer to question, *"Why am I here?"* The answer to that question is ***"For a purpose!"***

During one of his rousing speeches, Dr. Martin Luther King, Jr., summarized what he hoped others would state at his funeral. The essence of his comments was that he wanted to be remembered for the purpose of serving others. He stated, "I'd like somebody to mention that day that Martin Luther King, Jr. tried to give his life serving others. I'd like for somebody to say that day that Martin Luther King, Jr. tried to love somebody." All of us have a purpose and that purpose involves caring for, serving, and loving others.

So how do you realize the purpose that God has for you? One of the keys is to first realize that you are valuable. You are a unique creation of God, and He has a will for your life.

Because you are valuable to God, it is important to be yourself—even if no one praises you or acknowledges your value. You can meditate on verses such as Psalm 139:14–15 where we read, "I will praise You, for I am fearfully and wonderfully made . . . . My frame was not hidden from You, when I was made in secret . . . ." You can find assurance in Jeremiah 1:5, which states, "Before I formed you in the womb I knew you . . . ."

Because you are valuable, God will never leave you. Jeremiah 29:11 states, "For I know the thoughts that I think toward you, says the LORD, thoughts of peace and not of evil, to give you a future and a hope." God will prosper you and bring you to an expected end. He specializes in transforming a zero into a hero, nothing into something, nobody into somebody.

Because you are valuable, your spiritual enemy, Satan, seeks to destroy you. Our spiritual enemy, however, will not prevail against us. In Psalm 66:3 we read, "Say to God, 'How awesome are Your works! Through the greatness of Your power, Your enemies shall submit themselves to You.'"

You are so valuable that you are likened to an eagle. Isaiah 40:31 reminds us that the strength of those who wait on the Lord will be renewed: "But those who wait on the LORD shall renew *their* strength. They shall mount up with wings like eagles. They shall run and not be weary. They shall walk and not faint." Like the eagle, you *can have your strength renewed, see to seize opportunities, use the storm as a stepping stone to get to a destination, and can survive in the rocks of the mountains.* Just as the eagle is mighty and valuable among birds, so are you among people.

You are unique. You are divinely designed. No one is like you. You are different from everyone else in the world. The reason you are going through persecution, opposition from your neighbors and even your friends, is because of your uniqueness and value to God. For the sake of God's purpose for your life, do not let adversity overcome you.

Unlike the world, God values each of us for who we truly are—as the person He created us to be. Romans 12:6–8 reminds us that we each have differing gifts and that we are to use those gifts accordingly: "Having then gifts differing according to the grace that is given to us, *let us use them: if* prophecy, *let us prophesy* in proportion to our faith; or ministry, *let us use it* in *our* ministering; he who teaches, in teaching; he who exhorts, in exhortation; he who gives, with liberality; he who leads, with diligence; he who shows mercy, with cheerfulness."

Because you are a person of great value, I challenge you to not judge your value by what you are doing. Instead I encourage you to focus on your character and not compare yourself to others. Learn your strengths and identify your weaknesses. Run your own race instead of trying to keep pace with those in the lanes beside you. Know that your uniqueness is special to God and find security and assurance in His place for you. Know that God values you in ways that other people may not even see.

Of all the things that may remind you of your value, nothing surpasses the fact that Jesus Christ died on the cross on your behalf. His great sacrifice provided the way of your salvation. Salvation encompasses grace, redemption, and deliverance. Romans 8:32 states, "He that spared not his own Son, but delivered him up for us all, how shall he not with him also freely give us all things?"

A beautiful passage from Colossians 1:13-14 emphasizes the value God places on delivering His children: "He has delivered us from the power of darkness and conveyed us into the kingdom of the Son of His love, in whom we have redemption through His blood, the forgiveness of sins." Your value is underscored by the willingness of a holy God to disarm the powers and authorities, making a public spectacle of them and triumphing over them.

His blood makes you valuable. Through Hebrews 9:11-14 we learn more about the preciousness of the blood of Jesus Christ that was shed for us:

> But Christ came as High Priest of the good things to come, with the greater and more perfect tabernacle not made with hands, that is, not of this creation. Not with the blood of goats and calves, but with His own blood He entered the Most Holy Place once for all, having obtained eternal redemption. For if the blood of bulls and goats and the ashes of a heifer, sprinkling the unclean, sanctifies for the purifying of the flesh, how much more shall the blood of Christ, who through the eternal Spirit offered Himself without spot to God, cleanse your conscience from dead works to serve the living God?

Realizing your value, what should you do? How should you approach life? The answer is in the example of the Lord Jesus. Philippians 2:5-11 illustrates for us the "mind of Christ":

> Let this mind be in you which was also in Christ Jesus, who, being in the form of God, did not consider it robbery to be equal with God, but made Himself of no reputation, taking the form of a bondservant, and coming in the likeness of men. And being found in appearance as a man, He humbled Himself and became obedient to the point of death, even the death of the cross. Therefore God also has highly exalted Him and

given Him the name which is above every name, that
at the name of Jesus every knee should bow, of those
in heaven, and of those on earth, and of those under the
earth, and that every tongue should confess that Jesus
Christ *is* Lord, to the glory of God the Father.

Notice how the name of Jesus takes command; it does not bring dis-grace, shame, or embarrassment. Jesus had a settled identity instead of an identity crisis. He did not need people's approval and such is the case with those who have a settled identity. Jesus also has a settled sense of ownership. He knows what He has. He is the King of kings, and He does not have to fight for what is His own. Jesus also models for us a sense of settled position. Similarly, we do not need to put someone down to make ourselves look good. We should not manipulate to get to the top.

As a valuable person, you will keep producing. An example from Scripture is that of an unlikely animal—a spider! Proverbs 30:28 states that "the spider skillfully grasps with its hands, and it is in kings' palaces." Like the spider, a valuable person can keep on producing. The repro-ductive system of the spider is complex. During pregnancy, the spider changes its skin eleven different times. The pregnancy is lengthy. The female lays between fifty to a hundred eggs. As soon as the young spiders hatch, they are able to spin and eat prey. They are immediately productive.

Valuable people are productive. If they can't run, they walk. If they can't walk, they crawl. But, they make progress!

A valuable person knows his or her moment. The locust, a class of grasshopper, is a straight-winged insect. It travels for miles in the air, even though it cannot fly. Its wings are very narrow. The strength of the locust is not in the wings, but in the feet. The locust cannot fly, but it can jump. It jumps 200 times its height to propel itself. The locust waits for the wind to blow. Then it springs up and the wind carries it for miles. As the locust, *you* should know your moment. No one will tell you, but when it comes, you will know it. You will spring upward.

As a valuable person, you have the capacity to change challenges into opportunities. Everyone has challenges in life. Life is a continuous succession of problems and troubles History shows that problems are normal and will not end with you. Every rose is beautiful, but with the rose, comes the thorn.

The Old Testament example of Joseph serves as a great reference point for us. In Genesis 47:9, Joseph's father, Jacob, said to Pharaoh: "The days of the years of my pilgrimage are one hundred and thirty years;

few and evil have been the days of the years of my life, and they have not attained to the days of the years of the life of my fathers in the days of their pilgrimage." Similarly, in Job 14:1, we read, "Man who is born of woman is of *few days and full of trouble*."

Despite the problems in life that he faced, Joseph turned envy and hatred, slavery and prison into deliverance. We read about his problems and his victory over them in Psalm 105:17-20: "He sent a man before them—Joseph—who was sold as a slave. They hurt his feet with fetters. He was laid in irons. Until the time that his word came to pass, the word of the LORD tested him. The king sent and released him. The ruler of the people let him go free."

"He sent a man before them—Joseph—who was sold as a slave. They hurt his feet with fetters. He was laid in irons. Until the time that his word came to pass, the word of the LORD tested him. The king sent and released him. *The ruler of the people let him go free*." Later, after Joseph had the opportunity to exact vengeance on his brothers, we read that he acknowledged whatever ill treatment they intended was turned into an opportunity for God to develop Joseph's character: "But as for you, you meant evil against me; but *God meant it for good*, in order to bring it about as it is this day, to save many people alive" (Genesis 50:20).

Moses turned slavery and the death of his father and mother into safety: "He sent Moses His servant, and Aaron whom He had chosen. They performed His signs among them, and *wonders in the land of Ham*" (Psalm 105:26-27).

David in the desert, changed loneliness into victory: "And Saul said to David, 'You are not able to go against this Philistine to fight with him; for you *are* a youth, and he a man of war from his youth.' But David said to Saul, 'Your servant used to keep his father's sheep, and when a lion or a bear came and took a lamb out of the flock, I went out after it and struck it, and delivered the lamb from its mouth; and when it arose against me, I caught *it* by its beard, and struck and killed it. Your servant has killed both lion and bear; and *this uncircumcised Philistine will be like one of them*, seeing he has defied the armies of the living God'" (I Samuel 17:33–36).

More recent examples from history illustrate to us that individuals who are assured of their purpose and position in life can accomplish great things, despite their circumstances. For example, Franklin Delano Roosevelt, from his wheelchair, was one of the most successful presidents of the United States. Helen Keller, born deaf, dumb and blind, was an avid reader and writer and became an international role model, committing herself to help the deaf and blind. Joni Eareckson Tada, paralyzed from the neck down as the result of a diving accident, has a powerful ministry to the disabled community. She has hosted radio programs, is a writer, is a skilled painter who makes strokes by holding her paintbrush in her mouth, and even drives a vehicle.

At the time I am writing this book, there is an evangelist in the USA traveling around the world preaching who was born with no hands or feet but can use his mobile phone, drive a car, use his computer, swim, shave his beard, and can play soccer. His name: Pastor Nick Vujicic. Life without limbs for him meant going from no limbs to no limits.

As a valuable person, you will not tell how strong the storm is; instead, you will tell the storm how strong God is!

Know that you are a valuable person. Don't be satisfied with the comfort of your present condition. Notice the resolve that emanates from Joshua 24:15: "And if it seems evil to you to serve the LORD, choose for yourselves this day whom you will serve, whether the gods which your fathers served that were on the other side of the River, or the gods of the Amorites, in whose land you dwell. But as for me and my house, we will serve the LORD."

Dream big and resist the negative influence that might come from others who put you dream down. Remember the great Bible example of Joseph. In Genesis 37:5, we read, "Now Joseph had a dream, and he told it to his brothers; and they hated him even more." It's unfortunate that others will sometimes try to influence our dreams negatively either intentionally or unintentionally. The Lord draws our attention to the possibilities that He can provide. "Then Elisha said, 'Hear the word of the LORD. Thus says the LORD: 'Tomorrow about this time a seah of fine flour shall be sold for a shekel, and two seahs of barley for a shekel, at the gate of Samaria.'" So an officer on whose hand the king leaned answered the man of God and said, 'Look, if the LORD would make windows in heaven, could this thing be?' And he said, 'In fact, you shall see *it* with your eyes, but you shall not eat of it'" (2 Kings 7:1-2).

Consider the great dream that God provided for Abraham: "Then He brought him outside and said, 'Look now toward heaven, and count the stars if you are able to number them.' And He said to him, 'So shall your descendants be.'" (Genesis 15:5)

As a valuable person, you can rest in the fact that what you sow you shall also reap: "Do not be deceived, God is not mocked; for whatever a man sows, that he will also reap" (Galatians 6:7).

Life is not a 100-yard dash. You and I need to prepare ourselves for the future. One day, our lives on earth will end. Our race is important, but those who will follow us need preparation as well. Mike Devries said, "If there is no one to pass the baton to after my time as a leader, then I have not succeeded." Success without a successor is a profound failure. Harvey Firestone said, "The only way you can succeed permanently is when you help others to succeed." Achievement comes when people can do great things for *themselves*. Significance comes when a leader develops others to do great things *for* him. Success comes when a leader allows others to do great things *with* him. Legacy comes when he develops great organizations to do great things *without* him. What will be your legacy?

Regardless of your past and your present circumstances, accept that you are a valuable person. God has a purpose for you. Like me, you have survived to this point for purpose. Seek that purpose, find it, and live it!

CHAPTER FOURTEEN

TRIALS AND CHARACTER DEVELOPMENT

I thank God that He gives second chances. In reflecting on my life, I see that the trials the Lord brought into my life were for the purpose of character development. My plans were changed. War disrupted my life, the lives of my family members, and the lives of many others. The world as I knew it changed in a way that many would describe as completely negative. But the Lord is faithful.

The Lord orchestrated events in my life that gave me the opportunity to develop character. To identify the purpose He had for me, I had to be flexible and persevere. Even though I was a born again believer and serving in my local church, I did not want to be a minister of the gospel until the war came in 1989. Hiding under by bed and crying out to the Lord from Psalm 91, I asked the Lord to save me so I could serve Him for the rest of my life. I did not know how those words that I meant sincerely would come to pass. My ambition had been to become a medical doctor, not to be involved in ministry.

When I fled from Liberia shortly after war came to Monrovia, my focus remained on survival. I did not have time to reflect on the significance of the disruption of war to my education. Also, at that time, I had no idea that the war would last so long. When I was in Freetown as a refugee, many things ran as normal, even though the Civil War continued in Liberia and had spread to some of the remote parts of Sierra Leone. During that period of time in Freetown survival was not a daily preoccupation of mine. Over time, I became more aware—painfully at times—of the impact of war on my educational goals.

There were many times when I was discouraged and wanted to give up. It seemed at many points that there was no future for me. Everything seemed to be going wrong at times, and I could not see any opportunity for the future. Due to war, my education had to be hindered and there was no money to even continue if colleges or schools reopened. For a while, the future appeared dark. I felt at times that I was just gazing at each day as it came and went.

As early as 1991 some of my former friends and classmates participated in the UN resettlement program. As participants in that program, they were able to leave Africa and continue their education in the USA or in Europe. That program was available to all Liberian refugees, provided they had someone to serve as a contact person in the destination country. At that time, my older sister lived in Trenton, NJ. With an affidavit from her indicating my identity and relationship to her I could have participated in the resettlement program.

Many of my friends encouraged me to participate, like them, in the resettlement program because of the many opportunities such as housing, medical support, education, etc. At that time, however, I served as a volunteer at the Freetown Bible Training Center where I was enrolled as a student. In my mind, I did not feel that leaving abruptly to depart for the USA or Europe would honor the Lord and my commitment to serve.

As my friends continued to pressure me to take advantage of the opportunities of the resettlement program, I faced a tough decision. I envisioned them as successful medical doctors, consultants with the UN, engineers, lawyers, politicians, and business executives. I knew that they would enjoy the new life and opportunities that awaited them. Then, I envisioned myself as future doctor, meeting with patients in the hospital, having consultations, diagnosing sicknesses, and providing treatment.

Despite the difficulty of the decision and the temptations that accompanied it, I had peace that staying and serving in the FBTC was the right thing to do. I prayed about this decision and felt that God would have me to stay. There were plenty of opportunities to serve Him in Africa and the needs were many. I remembered the commitment to serve the Lord that I had made in 1990.

Over the years I have found encouragement by reading many books of people who had experienced discouragement and disappointment. I learned that God intervened in many of those situations to take what seemed bad and make it good. In my life, I have seen that God's purposes are far better than my narrow thinking. Some of the individuals who participated in the resettlement program went on to become highly successful. At times, hearing about their success makes me temporarily question my decision. But that line of thinking is very brief, because I know that I made the right decision.

Reading inspiring quotations has been an encouragement to me to not quit or give up. I am reminded to press on in serving the Lord based on decisions that I have made. A few quotes come to mind that have motivated me. Thomas Edison stated, "Many of life's failures are people who did not realize how close they were to success when they gave up." Another inspiring statement is from Albert Einstein: "In the midst of difficulties, that is when you find the greatest opportunities." I also like this quote from Dale Carnegie: "Most of the important things in life were accomplished by people who kept trying when there seems to be no hope."

Looking back, I see that the Lord enabled me to draw strength from His Word as well as from my experiences and the experiences of others. Making a long-term commitment is always difficult and there are many temptations to give up. Many years have passed since I committed fully to serving the Lord. Periodically, a question may emerge from myself or others regarding whether I made the right decision. But, I have learned to manage those thoughts and emotions over time. Each time I choose to press on despite adversity, my commitment is strengthened. I am reminded of the inspiring attitude of Benjamin Solomon Carson who wrote the following in *Gifted Hands: The Ben Carson Story:*

> "Success is determined not by whether or not you face
> obstacles, but by your reaction to them. And if you look
> at these obstacles as a containing fence, they become
> your excuse for failure. If you look at them as a hurdle,
> each one strengthens you for the next."

Most importantly, my faith shapes my response to life's major disappointments. I am totally convinced that without my faith in God I could not have made it through all the conflicts of war and the personal challenges I have faced. The Bible declares in Hebrews 11:6 (NKJV) that "without faith it is impossible to please God. He that comes to God must believe that He is and is the rewarder of those who diligently seek him." Through faith, my hopelessness was replaced with hope. In addition, the Lord has given me the opportunity to contribute positively in the lives of others.

Indeed, the Lord has blessed me in spite of adversity, including the disruption of my education. Time revealed to me that God had better purposes for me than my own plans and that my discouragement must give way to determination. That lesson—the most difficult aspect of my education—had to be learned through suffering. In the midst of that suffering, God had a better purpose for me: to live by the commitment that I made when I was under my bed and prayed to Him.

In the refiner's fire of character development, we learn that our lives are shaped as part of a process, just as gold is refined through its purification. Gold goes through a process to become attractive. The raw gold goes to the goldsmith, and it is heated so the impurities can be removed. The goldsmith watches carefully to make sure the gold does not overheat and become ruined. Finally, when the gold has been purified, it reflects like a mirror.

God is a refiner who works to reveal what we could not be without Him. When God wants to refine us, He will allow us to pass through things we do not expect. He allows the heat to separate the usable from the unusable. The trials we face in life enable the impurities to be removed so that finally others can see in us a reflection of the Lord Jesus.

God is the One who decides how long our refining will last. It may last from one week to many years. He refined Joseph from the time he was seventeen years old until he was 30 years old. It does not matter how long the refining takes; we come out refined. The molten gold does not have a shape after refining. The hot liquid will not take shape until it has cooled. When God has finished refining us, we have shape. We do not determine the mold; God will make us what He wants us to be.

Our trials refine us. Scripture reminds us of this testing process: "But He knows the way that I take; when He has tested me, I shall come forth as gold" Job 23:10 (NLJV). In response to our trials, we can become what God wants to become. Consider the example of a caterpillar turning into a beautiful butterfly, wheat becoming a wholesome loaf of bread, or the combination of sodium and chloride becoming table salt.

Hebrews 12:2 gives us the example that we can look to when we need to persevere through difficult circumstances. In that verse, we read, "Looking unto Jesus, the author and finisher of our faith, who for the joy that was set before Him endured the cross, despising the shame, and has sat down at the right hand of the throne of God" Hebrews 12:2 (NKJV). Notably, that verse links future joy with temporary suffering. Our trials are temporary; but our joy can be permanent.

When Bishop Polycarp was arrested by Emperor Nero and tied to the stick to be burned, Nero threatened him and said, "Denounce Jesus and I will not burn you." But Bishop Polycarp, 87 years old, said that he had served Jesus and had never been disappointed. He said he could not denounce Him. He said, "You threaten me with a fire that burns temporarily, but Jesus will bring a fire that burns eternally." Then he concluded with, "I have come too far; I cannot turn back."

God will bring us out after the refining. The gold is put in the refinery because of the desired outcome. Similarly, we go into the refining process as raw material, and we come out a finished product. We go from the furnace to the showcase!

One of the keys to living a victorious spiritual life is to recognize that the trials we face are part of the process of God developing our character. Many of our life experiences are out of our control. We cannot decide who our parents will be, the country where we are born, the color of our skin, or our native language. Nor can we determine if our lives will be subject to the ravages of war and the brutal violence that plagues many nations. Regardless, we can respond in faith and experience God's refining in our lives as He develops our character.

The development of character is a topic I hear discussed often due to my involvement in ministry. Along with that topic, I also hear discussions of charisma in relation to character. Many people have charisma, which is the ability to have an attractive and magnetic personality or style. Unfortunately, many with charisma lack character. My observation is that while charisma may take you to the mountaintop, only character will keep you there.

Character is the real you. It's your behavior, your attitude, and in general, who you are when no one is watching. Character and integrity go together. *Integrity* is taken from the Latin word *integer,* which means complete or whole. Job 27:5 states, "Until I die, I will not deny my integrity." That verse challenges us to focus on wholeness.

Character is living out the message you preach or the values you project as your own. A minister might deliver a message eloquently, but the real test is whether the minister lives the message he preaches. The extent of the congruence that links what we say and what we do and what we hold dear reveals the depth of our integrity. Our character and integrity affect how we view God's Word, how we handle money, regard possessions, interact with others, and serve as stewards of our influence.

Maybe your charisma and your character are not complementing each other. The Lord Jesus can fix that. Peter denied Jesus. He failed in character and charisma! Yet, after the resurrection, the angel told the disciples go and tell Peter and the other disciples about the empty tomb. Peter messed up, but Jesus changed his mess into a miracle. You might think your situation is beyond repair, but God can make good of any situation.

In life, we all start somewhere and end somewhere (Job 23:10). Where we end is related to our character development. Not all of us start at the same level, nor do we determine where we start. Fortunately, our value is not determined by our lot in life. By God's grace, he can transform the circumstances and the situations in which we find ourselves. If we don't move forward or if we quit because of obstacles that we face, we won't progress anywhere. Our character development will stall. Along our journey, we can expect to face some setbacks and failures. We can find encouragement in knowing that everyone experiences failures. Our goal is to keep moving, gaining knowledge, growing spiritually, and increasing in character.

Although we cannot control many of the variables at work in our lives, we can control our behavior. Our behavior reveals the picture we have of ourselves. Our behavior will make or break us. We can only blame ourselves if our behavior is not in line with our values. Galatians 6:6–7 reminds us that we will reap what we sow. The relationship between sowing and reaping, referred to as the law of the harvest, will not change. We must change to align with the law of the harvest. As we continue to develop character, we will eventually see a causal relationship between our behavior and the resulting positive rewards that we reap.

Unfortunately, there are many influences in our lives that hinder our character development and threaten our integrity. In the account of Job, even Job's wife—seeing only the negative—discouraged her husband. In Job 2:9 (NKJV), we read, "Then his wife said to him, 'Do you still hold fast to your integrity? Curse God and die!' Job said, 'You are talking like a foolish woman.'" Job's commitment to faithfulness was rewarded in the end. His character developed much. He reaped the benefits of responding in faith to the trials that he could not have prevented in his life.

Job had to wait to see how God would resolve the negative circumstances of his life. From my own experience, I am convinced that the ability to be faithful and to wait on the Lord determines whether we will meet God or miss some opportunity that could be pivotal in life. Our commitment must be to the Lord and His purposes. Our intent must be to trust the Lord fully with our lives. God expects us to be patient, consistent, remain in a state of expectancy, to be ready for what comes our way, and to endure in spite of adversity.

Even through the horrors of war, the Lord opened up opportunities for me. Just one example is the opportunity He provided for me to attend a Bible school in Sierra Leone. The Lord then enabled me to serve in ministry in my local church. We all face conflicts and difficulties that on the surface appear to be only negative. But God is faithful, and He desires that we will be faithful as well. When I committed to the Lord in prayer to serve Him, I made a pledge that I should not forget. Character development demands that I continue forward, despite the hardships. In so doing our trials become the basis for continued development of our character. Our character can then honor and bring glory to Him.

Thank God that He will always bring people into our lives who will help us to develop spiritually and grow in character. As I interact with others there are some things that I try **not** to do. I try not to allow pride to enter in when people give compliments or praise. I try not to speak out if I'm confused. I try not to overreact when others offend me. I try not to speak critically of others. I try not to become enamored with money, power, or desire. I try not to become jealous of others. I try not to encourage others to give or share if I'm not willing to do the same.

On the other hand, there are things that I try diligently to do as part of my character development. I try to go to the Lord humbly prayer in all matters. I try to maintain character for the glory of God. I try to measure success by faithfulness in spiritual matters. I try to respect and help others with an open, caring, and generous attitude. I try to exercise wisdom in relationships. I try to accept myself and giftings as I am and not compete with others. I try to promote teamwork with others.

The greatest resource that we have for character development is the Bible. One thing that will establish us strongly to finish our journey is studying and meditating on God's Word. There is tremendous, miraculous power in God's Word. Isaiah 40:8 (NKJV) reminds us that ". . . the word of God stands forever." The Lord Jesus taught that we are not to live by bread alone but ". . . by every word that proceeds from the mouth of God" (Matthew 4:4). We also know from Scripture that the word of God is ". . . a discerner of the thoughts and intents of the heart" (Hebrews 4:12). In relation to studying Scripture, the Apostle Paul admonishes diligence so that we may be workers who ". . . rightly divide the word of truth" 2 Timothy 2:15 (NKJV). Those passages show us that the Bible is to be our source and our guide. If we are students of the Bible, then we will be much better prepared to interpret our trials appropriately in light of God's purposes. Those insights will help us develop character.

There are many passages from Scripture that can help us put difficult times into proper perspective. One example is Romans 8:31–32, which states: "What then shall we say to these things? If God *is* for us, who can be against us? He who did not spare His own Son, but delivered Him up for us all, how shall He not with Him also freely give us all things?" Those verses assure us that God's love protects us and that He provides for us as evidenced by the sacrifice of the Lord Jesus for our redemption.

As incredible as Romans 8:31–32 (NKJV) is, we read later in that same chapter (verses 37–39) that nothing can separate us from the love of Christ: "Yet in all these things we are more than conquerors through Him who loved us. For I am persuaded that neither death nor life, nor angels nor principalities nor powers, nor things present nor things to come, nor height nor depth, nor any other created thing, shall be able to separate us from the love of God which is in Christ Jesus our Lord." Who shall separate us from the love of Christ? In *all* things—trouble, hardship, famine, nakedness, danger, sword, death, life, angels or demons—we are more than conquerors! We are assured that if we put our faith in the Lord, that we will be able to experience the refiner's fire, and we will be the better for it!

I have much to learn in life, but I have learned some important lessons. One lesson that enables me to make sense of the experiences of my life is to understand that my response to the trials I face determines the extent of my character development. Just after Christmas in 2007, I faced a major trial that affected our entire family.

My wife, daughter Rebekah, and niece Rugiatu were traveling on December 28, 2007, from Kenema to Freetown in a vehicle with plate number ADK 851. At about 12:30 p.m. they left Bo for Freetown. Just outside of Bo, a town called Senehun, a boy tried to cross the road. The driver was speeding and he tried to dodge the boy. At first the boy moved in one direction but then he shifted toward the vehicle. Due to the speed and how close the vehicle was to the boy, the vehicle struck the boy. Unfortunately, the boy died instantly. After hitting the boy, the vehicle flew into a large drainage area with a concrete wall. The impact immediately stopped the vehicle, but the carrier on top flew off and struck and girl and a man, killing both of them. All ten people in the vehicle (nine passengers plus the driver) were wounded severely. Many hands and feet were broken and some had deep cuts.

Those involved were transported to the Bo government hospital. At the time, I was in Monrovia with my son Manasseh conducting a camp for young people offered through Hope Universal. Word of the accident reached Mariama's auntie in Bo, and she was able to relay a message to me through a couple of other contacts. My son and I left Monrovia and took a taxi to the Sierra Leonean border and from there another taxi to the hospital in Bo.

Our daughter Rebekah did not have a scratch on her body. Praise the Lord! This was a great miracle. Both of my wife's arms were broken in three locations and her right foot was broken. Rugiatu's hip was broken and her eyes were swollen shut due to the impact from the accident. The area surrounding her eyes was black due to bruising. When I saw both of them at the hospital, they still had blood on them. The staff at that hospital could only try to relieve the pain and temporarily place a splint on the broken bones.

My wife and niece badly needed medical treatment, but no ambulances were available, nor were any specialists in the area to treat the severe bone damage. They both needed to go to the hospital in Freetown. I called on a friend of mine who owned a Toyota truck. We paid for the fuel and with his help managed to have them transported to the Emergency hospital in the Goderich area of Freetown. We arrived there on December 31 at about 3:00 a.m.

Rugiatu regained her sight after about three days. Eventually, she could smile. Her broken hip began to mend. Mariama required much more extensive treatment. Nine surgeries were required for the insertion of metal plates and other treatment of her damaged bones. She remained in the emergency hospital for four months. Finally, she was discharged in April and came home in a wheelchair. She was to go back to the hospital after two weeks for a follow-up visit.

Because of the difficult terrain near our home in Konde Farm, a person must cross a river on stones to enter the area. No vehicle can reach this community because the bridge is incomplete. Four men carried my wife in the wheelchair up the hill to our house. That was the only way to transport her to our home. Two weeks later, four men had to carry the wheelchair across the river again to get to the place where she could get in a taxi. She remained in much pain for a long period of time and the situation was very difficult for her and our family.

Over time, she progressed from using the wheelchair to using a walker. She continued to visit the hospital every two weeks for a checkup and for physical therapy. Later she moved from the walker to using crutches. Then, after another month, she could walk with the help of only one crutch. Next, she improved to using only a small crutch. Later that year, in September of 2008, Mariama attended a special service

143

for women held at the Bethel Konde Farm church. During that time a lady came to minister who had an encouraging influence on Mariama. The two had met earlier and the lady who came to minister knew about Mariama's faith. She encouraged Mariama to begin walking without use of any crutch. Mariama prayerfully put that word into practice through faith. Today, she is walking without crutches. We thank God that He has restored her condition.

The one element of my life that is under my control is how I respond to the circumstances that I cannot control. As we progress through life, all of us must go through trials that do not seem fair. Often those trials involve difficulties that affect others, including those we love. Through all those difficulties, we can rest assured that God has a purpose for our lives and He is interested in refining our character.

CHAPTER FIFTEEN

KONDE FARM AND MINISTRY OUTREACH

W hen I met with Mark Stewart in Anderson, SC, in 2002, I became intrigued by his ideas for a new ministry that came to be known as Hope Universal. The trip was my first to the U.S. and resulted from my invitation to speak at the Gideons International Convention in Louisville, KY, in 2002. When Mark learned that I was in Atlanta visiting my sister following the convention, he invited me to meet with him in Anderson. I agreed and he bought my bus ticket.

Interestingly, I met with Mark the same year that the war officially ended in Sierra Leone (2002). During my meeting with Mark, I learned about Mark's plans to form a non-profit missions organization that would provide both physical and spiritual help for people in need. Of particular interest at that time were the people who had endured years of brutal violence in Sierra Leone. Mark had witnessed firsthand the incredible devastation to the country and he wanted to assist. My commitment to serve the Lord had led me in many directions. Working with Hope Universal seemed like the next appropriate step.

When I returned to Sierra Leone in 2002, I began working on forming Hope Universal Sierra Leone. We had no office, so we held meetings at my house in Malama, located near Freetown. Our initial outreach efforts mainly involved showing *The JESUS Film* and coordinating conferences for church pastors and leaders. The ministry of Hope Universal Sierra Leone began to grow. From that time forward, the outreach of Hope Universal has expanded in Sierra Leone. In addition, we also extended the ministry efforts of the Hope Universal in to Liberia. That initiative is now called Hope for Liberia.

An amazing expansion of the role of Hope Universal in Sierra Leone occurred when my wife and I moved in 2004. We moved to a place called Konde Farm (pronounced Kondee and sometimes spelled Kondie). The way the Lord orchestrated that move and my wife's instrumentality in the decision deserve some explanation.

We had been renting in Malama an area near Freetown that is about a 25-minute walk from Konde Farm. In Malama, we lived in a decent house but it was very expensive. Water was limited, so we had to buy water to cook and for laundry, etc. My wife, Mariama, discovered that others were going to the Marimbo River near Konde Farm to do their laundry. She investigated the situation and liked what she saw, especially compared to having to buy water. Even though the Marimbo River required Mariama to walk about 25 minutes each way, she began washing our clothes in that river.

During that period, we were troubled by the stress of paying rent. In Africa, a full year's rent is paid in advance. Making that payment meant that for months, we had to go without items we needed. Adding to the financial stress, our landlord, a military man, tended to threaten us. He told us that if we did not pay the rent he would make us regret the decision. When the time came near to pay the rent, our stress levels rose considerably.

In 2004, we gathered up the rent money for the year and traveled to pay our landlord. He and his wife lived near military barracks. When we arrived, I got out of the taxi and held the black plastic bag containing the rent money. My wife offered to help me. I handed her the bag. In a flash, she went over to another taxi and got in. The taxi drove off before I even knew what was happening. My wife took all of the rent money and left!

Of course, my wife's action confused me. We had already told the landlord that we were bringing the money. I proceeded in to meet him, but he was not there. I told his wife that we had come to pay but that something had happened. She said, "Well, you can pay later." I took a taxi back home where I planned to ask my wife some important questions.

When I arrived back home, I asked my wife why she had taken the money and returned home in a taxi without me. She said, "I'm tired of living here as if we are in bondage, living only to pay rent." She felt the stress from renting was not healthy since we needed to send our two children to school. Although she expressed her feelings about the situation, she refused to tell me where she put the money.

The rent was due in March, but Mariama kept the money well into April. Fortunately, the landlord knew that we paid regularly, so they allowed a little extra time. I told my wife that keeping the money and not paying our rent was dangerous because we could get evicted. I also reminded her of the previous threats from our landlord. Another concern of mine was damage to my reputation in relation to ministry. When I expressed these concerns to my wife, she simply laughed! My concerns and frustration grew.

As the situation progressed, I went to my pastor to seek his help and guidance. He and his wife visited our home. During our discussion of the matter, my wife finally said, "If you want to know where the money is, I will show you." Of course, we indicated our interest. She led us outside and said that we would have to go on a walk. We followed her.

My wife led us to Konde Farm. After walking 25 minutes or so to get there, my curiosity was at the breaking point. I had never visited Konde Farm. Then my wife pointed to a piece of land and said, "The money is with that land. I paid a deposit in advance for that land. We will not have to rent anymore."

Imagine my shock! My wife had taken our rent money and made a deposit on land in Konde Farm. She had given the Muslim chief of Konde Farm all of our rent money for the year as the deposit. In Sierra Leone, I could not own land in my name because I was a citizen of Liberia, not Sierra Leone. Mariama had learned about the availability of the land during her visits to the area to wash clothes in the Marimbo River. She had talked to the chief and had later made the deposit. The deposit amounted to about 2/3 of the total cost of the land, which covered two town lots. (A town lot is one tenth of an acre.)

As I considered the words and actions of my wife, my pastor said, "This is a big blessing." He commented on the advantages of owning land in Konde Farm rather than renting in Malama. Up to that time, I had not been happy. Suddenly, satisfaction overcame me as evidenced by a big smile and the appreciation I had for my wife.

We moved out of the rented home in Malama and placed many of our belongings with others. We did so in haste because the landlord's wife heard that we might be moving out of the house we had been renting. She came to the house one day and inquired. I explained the situation to her and apologized. She told us to leave at once. Then we temporarily moved into the office in the Great Commission building that I had access to due to my ministry work.

We stayed in that office while we built a one-room house on the land at Konde Farm. Some of my family members helped us financially so that we could pay the remainder of what we owed for the land. During that time of building our house in Konde Farm we established a relationship with the chief that would prove to be important later.

Konde Farm is the village where the Lord has strategically placed us. I am committed to continuing to serve the Lord there and to try to expand our ministry outreach. Our move to Konde Farm in 2004 led to our developing a relationship with the chief. We also became aware of the ministry needs in that predominantly Muslim area. One request I had was for Hope Universal to offer a medical clinic there.

In February 2006, Hope Universal conducted a free medical clinic at Konde Farm. The clinic was held for three days and about 1,000 people (mostly Muslim) were treated free of charge. The clinic's medical staff included Mark Stewart's father-in-law (Kunjappan John) and mother-in-law (Vimala John), both medical doctors from India; a nurse from Seneca, SC, named Jane Chupp; and Joe Bacher, from Westminster, SC, who served as the Emergency Medical Technician. Other staff included Mark Stewart, Larry Reeves, Kent McGahey, and Greg Vieau, all from Concord Community Church in Anderson, SC.

At the time Hope Universal offered the medical clinic in 2006, there was no school or church at Konde Farm. The Muslim people there were in great need of educational support and medical services. The large crowds who showed up for the medical clinic were handled with a specific plan. A ticket was issued to each individual. With a ticket, an individual could progress through a defined sequence of services. First, a nurse checked vitals. Second, the participant saw a doctor. Third, the participant went to the pharmacy on site. Finally, each participant was able to meet with a person for counseling services. Many of the participants in this medical clinic gave their lives to the Lord Jesus.

The medical clinic at Konde Farm was a great success physically and spiritually. I remember Larry Reeves asking me a question following the close of the clinic. He asked, "Now that so many people have gotten saved, what are we going to do?" Then he asked, "Do you think we could start a church here." I said, "Yes, but there is no building available."

The only building available was a stick building at the top of a mountain on the outskirts of Konde Farm. That mountain top was extremely difficult to reach. Larry Reeves and I walked there. First, we had to go through a thickly forested area. Then we had to climb up steep terrain with difficulty. That walk to the mountain top proved fruitful because we decided to start holding services there. Later, on March 5, 2006, we held the first service at Konde Farm Sanctuary of Empowerment Bethel Church. At that time, we used the temporary stick building atop the mountain.

First church at Konde Farm

Later, we asked the chief of Konde Farm if he would give us a place to hold church services. Although the chief is a Muslim, he saw that we were having a positive effect in Konde Farm through the medical clinic and the church meetings. Prior to the outreach efforts in Konde Farm, there was a lot of drinking, disruption, and confusion. The presence of the church in the area had helped those situations. By that time, we had also planned a summer school, which promised to be a great help to the community. The chief allowed us to use on a temporary basis some land that he owned. The chief was open to and seemed supportive of our efforts.

We used the land the chief had given access to for the church building location. We built a stick building and put zinc (tin) on it for a roof. We held our first services there in May 2006. We began promoting the school that we wanted to launch that summer. When we had enough participants, we opened the summer school in late June 2006.

We continued holding church services and school meetings on the temporary property the chief had granted to us. By 2007, the chief had seen more positive effects of the church and school at Konde Farm. He then offered to give us land for free on a permanent basis for the purposes of having a church, a medical clinic, and a school for grades kindergarten through eleventh. The size of the property is two town lots (a town lot is one tenth of an acre). The chief had noticed the growth and positive social and spiritual effects. His doing this as a Muslim is remarkable.

The land that the chief deeded to us was rocky and sloping, so it was not the best land in the Konde Farm area. Needless to say, we were pleased to have this donated land. On that land, with the help of Hope Universal, Concord Community Church, and Konde Farm Sanctuary of Empowerment Bethel Church, a church building was erected. Next came construction of the medical clinic building. Finally, the school building was constructed. Those buildings occupied nearly all of the two town lots. Currently, the church, the medical clinic, and the school building are used on a regular basis and are functioning successfully. We are grateful for the many individuals who have donated funds for these efforts, including the one individual who provided the funds for the building of the medical clinic.

In addition to the ministry efforts at Konde Farm, in 2008 Hope Universal launched a Bible school for church leaders needing more training to be effective in ministry. The Bible school started with one campus at the Scripture Union Hall in Freetown. The Bible school is set up for a three-year curriculum. The first year is focused on discipleship. Year two emphasizes leadership and evangelism. Year three is focused on missions. Students are not charged any fees. Those who attend return to their churches to carry out the vision of their respective churches. My role is to help set the direction of the Bible school. There is a coordinator and teachers at each school. Hope Universal helps provide honoraria for teachers and assists with their transportation costs. Some assistance for students to attend is available as needed.

As enrollment in the Bible school grew, we needed more classroom space. To accommodate expansion, we secured use of the Bethel Bible College in Freetown. Use of that facility provided more classroom space for the Bible school. We started other campuses at Wilberforce and at Konde Farm. Each year we hold a Bible school graduation in the last week of June or the first week in July. Our graduates are from various churches in Sierra Leone and represent different churches and denominations.

Many people have been amazed at the progress of Hope Universal in Sierra Leone. Most people did not think that our moving to Konde Farm would work out as well as it did, but we praise God that He guided us in that process. During the dedication of the medical clinic in 2010, over 400 people showed up, including the Muslim chief of Konde Farm and representatives from the U.S. from Concord Community Church and Hope Universal. Larry Reeves addressed the crowd with a speech about how the whole process started. When it was time for chief Konde Kargbo to speak, he said, "No one else has made an impact in the life of this village like what you have done here."

Church, school, clinic and well at Konde Farm

Hearing the words from a Muslim chief 20 years after I prayed under a bed in Monrovia, moved me emotionally. I was reminded that those who continue in their commitment to the Lord are never forsaken. God can use them to accomplish much for Him. For the chief to mention the unprecedented impact on the village was amazing. My mind was drawn back to asking the Lord to save me from dying in the war so that I could serve Him. Thinking about that moment in relation to the progress represented by the church, the medical clinic, the school, and the Bible school is a significant spiritual highlight for me.

The improvements at Konde Farm have been a positive influence in our ministry efforts. In my role as International Director of Hope Universal, one of the strategies the Lord has given me is to replicate in other countries what we have begun in Konde Farm. This approach is called the Hope Genesis Project.

We have seen the Hope Genesis Project work in another area: Gbainty Village within the Lungi area of Sierra Leone. Gbainty Village is a predominantly a Muslim village located on the northern part of Freetown. My wife and I have a friend named Jacob Gbateh who lives there. He invited us to conduct a church leader conference there in 2009-10. When I spoke at that conference about what Hope Universal is involved in at Konde Farm, Jacob requested similar assistance in Gbainty Village. In particular, he wanted to have a water project there due to the water needs.

I mentioned Jacob's request for a water project to Kent McGahey since Kent has an interest in assisting with drilling wells. Brother Kent had helped us previously in attempting to dig a well at Konde Farm. Those efforts did not work, however, due to the rocky terrain in the Konde Farm area. The rocks and stones prevented the successful completion of a well at Konde Farm. Also, in 2010 during a Hope Universal mission trip to Sierra Leone, Kent attempted to lead a well drilling project in Gbainty Village. Unfortunately, that effort was not successful either. The drilling equipment got stuck and the project had to end. Due to the circumstances, the equipment was covered and left there. But abandoning the equipment there was not a good testimony. Each time I saw Jacob Gbateh, he asked when we could resume the project.

When I took over as International Director of Hope Universal in January of 2013, I wanted to resume the well drilling project in Gbainty Village. Kent McGahey, Reynolds Holiman (an engineer from Florida), and Mark Stewart completed training in well drilling offered through Equip Ministries. Following the training, Reynolds took it upon himself to raise money for the well drilling project in Gbainty Village. In addition, we made plans and raised money for a well to be dug by hand in Konde Farm.

I visited the U.S. in February 2013. During that time, part of my emphasis was the promotion of the water projects at Gbainty Village and Konde Farm. Due to the excellent fundraising efforts of Reynolds, I focused mainly on raising money for the well project at Konde Farm.

The labor for the well digging by hand in Konde Farm began in March 2013. Digging by hand meant that laborers used equipment to manually dig and remove soil. When the workers encountered a stone while digging, they sent someone down the shaft to light a fire on the stone. After several days, the heat from the fire enabled the stone to begin to crack. The cracked stone then could be removed and the digging continued. The workers dug and removed stones in this manner for about two months. During that time period, Kent McGahey and Reynolds Holiman visited Sierra Leone as part of a mission trip. They were able to observe and support the project. They gave input and helped secure some of the supplies that would be needed to complete the project. By May 2013, the well diggers hit water and then they poured concrete from the bottom to top of the well shaft until the well was completed and a pump had been installed. That project was a success!

During their visit in April 2013, Kent and Reynolds also helped support the well drilling project in Gbainty Village. While the well drilling project was underway in Gbainty Village, Hope Universal also offered a free medical clinic. The medical clinic resulted in about 120 individuals obtaining treatment free of charge. While some staff worked with the medical clinic, others worked on the well drilling project, assisting the team conducting the drilling.

While the well drilling project was in progress, I had to travel to Monrovia to conduct a church leader conference, a youth camp, and a team completing a medical clinic. While in Liberia, I received the news that the well project in Gbainty Village was a success. In addition, the success of the medical clinic and the well drilling project strongly affected the chief of Gbainty Village. As a result of those projects and Jacob Gbateh's ministry efforts, the chief offered 10 town lots (1 acre) of land. The purpose of that land offer was to provide space for a church building, a medical clinic, and a school. As I write, Bible study is going on now in Gbainty Village. The ministry efforts are a partnership of Life Evangelical Ministry (led by Jacob Gbateh) and Hope Universal.

Our vision to expand ministry efforts by replicating what has been successful in Konde Farm is called the Genesis Project. That vision includes entering a new location and identifying land to use as a ministry base, starting a church, a school, and a medical clinic. Implementation would be based on the needs of the particular area or community. For example, in some areas a well may be needed more than a school or medical clinic.

The Genesis Project is a model that has been fruitful in Konde Farm and Gbainty Village. This approach shows that sharing the love of Christ through offering physical and spiritual help results in positive effects. I pray that ministry efforts like the Genesis Project will be replicated in other countries. From our strategic location in Konde Farm, I hope to be instrumental in continuing to provide physical and spiritual help in many other locations.

In August 2013, we made positive changes to our Bible school structure. Previously, we had one Bible school in the central part of Freetown (Pademba Road area). However, we realized that as enrollment increased, students experienced transportation problems due to the distances traveled to attend. As a result, we decentralized and created four additional Bible schools. Those are located in Konde Farm, Wilberforce, Kissy, and Lungi. As a result of ministry relationships in those areas, space for each Bible school as well as teaching ministers are available. Due to the decentralization, enrollment has increased from approximately 20 students to over 100.

In October 2013, Karlin Bacher, a registered nurse from Westminster, SC, relocated to Konde Farm. Brother Karlin's commitment to relocate to Konde Farm to open the medical clinic generated much excitement among Hope Universal staff as well as the people needing services. The goal was to operate the medical clinic on a weekly basis. One of the challenges encountered was trying to keep the clinic open only part-time each week. We realized that additional staff would be required to operate the medical clinic on a full-time basis.

Brother Karlin oversaw the medical clinic efforts for about six months. Then, in March 2014, he transitioned to a new opportunity. Since that time, we employed a doctor, two nurses, and one administrative staff member. Along with the help of other volunteers, the medical and administrative staff keep the clinic open from Monday through Saturday from 8:00 a.m. to 6:00 p.m. and on Sunday as needed (for emergencies). The expanded hours are helping provide access and services for the men, women, and children of Konde Farm and surrounding communities.

Another outreach we started in Sierra Leone is a modification of "Simply the Story," which is a ministry to people who are not literate. Bible teaching according to that model is based on dramatizing Bible stories and then soliciting volunteers from the audience to demonstrate understanding by acting out the main points of the story. Our modified outreach is called "Story Telling Ministry" (STM). A train the trainer workshop was held in November 2013, in Freetown, Sierra Leone. After launching that outreach in Sierra Leone, we held another train the trainer workshop in Monrovia, Liberia in December 2013. Currently, the STM outreaches continue in Sierra Leone and Liberia.

All of the ministries noted above were formed under the oversight of Hope Universal. In March 2014, the board of Hope Universal decided the time was right for a transition in structure. After years of serving in Sierra Leone and Liberia, Hope Universal transitioned from a funded staff approach to a missionary support approach. That transition resulted in a transfer of ministry responsibility from the oversight of Hope Universal to the African ministers of Sierra Leone and Liberia. Those ministers now function as missionaries who are responsible for raising their own support.

This approach will allow for long-term sustainability and will provide greater flexibility to respond quickly to community needs.

As a result of the transitions with Hope Universal, I will have additional time to devote to ministries such as holding church leader conferences in more African countries, planting churches, launching new Bible and regular schools, and coordinating the provision of scholarships for children whose parents cannot afford to pay for their education. There is also much need in the areas of children's homes and orphanages. Many children in West Africa either live homeless with their parents or live homeless on their own because their parents are dead. The needs are many.

CHAPTER SIXTEEN

LOOKING BACK
AND FORWARD

As I reflect on my life, I am reminded of the commitment I made in July 1990 as I lay under my bed and prayed to God that my family and I would survive. At that time, people in Monrovia were in a state of confusion about the conflicts that were occurring nearby. The rebels had advanced closer to the city and the AFL forces were split among troops defending the city and those engaging rebels on the front. During this time period, many of us underestimated the severity of the war that lay ahead. Having not lived through war before, many of us did not realize what war was like.

Before long, total confusion emerged as people went in all directions seeking refuge from the conflict. Even before the rebels reached the city of Monrovia, portions of the AFL committed acts of violence against Gios and Manos in the city. Part of the reason for the AFL violence in Monrovia was to avenge losses the Krahn AFL experienced against the mainly Gio and Mano rebels on the front. Witnessing the confusion in the city created fear and tension inside me. I knew surviving would be difficult for all of us.

When the rebels entered Monrovia, the church that I attended, St. Simon Baptist Church, held a prayer meeting. During the prayer meeting that involved multiple churches, we prayed that the Lord would bring an end to the violence. The prayer meeting occurred as fighting continued on the outskirts of Monrovia against the NPFL and AFL forces. AFL forces thought that we had gathered to pray on behalf of the rebels. As a result,

AFL soldiers began going from house to house committing violence and murder against civilians.

For days the AFL committed violence against civilians in Monrovia while at the same time the rebels advanced into the city. By that time, fighting occurred all around us. Hearing the sounds of the weapons along with screams and cries is unforgettable. I remember hearing people yell things such as, "Oh, I am dying." As the momentum of combat increased near our house, we closed the doors and put tables and chairs there for protection.

During that time of intense fighting in Monrovia, we all had to take cover. One night in particular, the fighting occurred especially close to our house. On that night I lay under my bed beside my brother. Due to fear of what might happen, I shivered as I listened to the sounds of combat. I prayed from Psalm 91 and experienced some hope through prayer. I prayed, "Lord if you deliver me from this war, I promise, I will serve you for the rest of my life." I asked the Lord to spare me for the purpose of living for Him and serving Him. That commitment to the Lord changed my life.

At that time I had been a believer for a number of years. When I was younger, my pastor used to tell me that one day the Lord would use me. I did not fully accept what my pastor told me. When I prayed that night in 1990, however, I cried out with the intensity brought on by the tension and fear of living close to death. In a way, my prayer was a confession. I believed in my heart that I had denied the Lord—at least partly—regarding serving Him fully. At that moment I had a clarification of commitment and a sincere willingness to serve Him, regardless of the circumstances.

I desired to survive until the war came to an end and to serve then. Perhaps because of my youthful lack of understanding, I did not realize that even within a time of war there are opportunities to minister. In my mind, as long as the war continued, everything would be at a standstill and I could not minister under those conditions. I later realized that this is not the case. Even during conflict, the opportunity to serve is great.

That encounter with God during my fervent prayer in 1990 has strengthened and energized me many times as I reflected on it. That defining moment has been a motivator to me to press on. Each time I remember it, I renew my commitment afresh. It represented a humble and complete willingness to seek God's will above my own. I had previously wanted to have my own way. But at that particular time, I was ready to give up my own will and control and do what the Lord wanted me to do.

That point in my life represented a continuation of dying to self and living for God. I believe all individuals who desire to walk with the Lord have a similar experience at some point. Over time, I have discussed a similar experience with others who have stopped seeking their own way. For example, I discussed this topic recently with a former professional football player in Florida. He reached a point where he completely yielded to God's will. This shared experience among believers is not exactly the same, but the essence of the encounter with God is the same. During those times, we realize our own weakness and the mighty strength of God. God reassures us as in Ephesians 2:10 that as believers he has a purpose for us and that we are his workmanship (handiwork). He has foreordained good works for us to walk in as we serve Him.

When I prayed my pledge to God in 1990, I thought that during war ministry would have to wait. I soon realized that opportunities to minister often come in the envelope of conflict. The Lord enabled me to serve in many capacities beginning with serving at Freetown Bible Training Center (FBTC) in 1992. From that time forward, God continued to open doors of ministry.

While serving as an administrator at FBTC, the RUF rebels in Sierra Leone continued their advance toward Freetown. As was the case in Monrovia, I lived in a capital city toward which rebel forces advanced. During that time, Liberians were often arrested and charged with being aligned with the rebels. As a result, many Liberians who had sought refuge in Sierra Leone left the country. I felt that God had opened up the opportunity for me to serve at the Bible school as an administrator. I could have left like other Liberians, but I remembered my commitment to the Lord. I decided to stay, despite the dangers. God protected me during that time, whereas many other Liberians were arrested, beaten, and placed in jail. I continued serving and felt that God protected me.

The Lord providentially enabled me to meet my wife while I was a refugee in Sierra Leone. God placed us in a missionary training school in 1996, where we met Mark Stewart, an American from Anderson, SC. At that time, neither Mark nor I knew how God would weave our lives together through Hope Universal.

By 1997, I had the opportunity to speak at a large pastors' conference involving approximately 600 pastors. From that point through 2001, I spoke at similar pastors' conferences. Those conferences were held in Sierra Leone behind rebel lines in Bo, Kenema, Kono, Port Loko, Makeni, Bonthe, and Moyamba. I also had the opportunity to speak at a larger pastors' conference. World Vision had been praying for 1,200 pastors from various churches to be able to attend a large conference. That conference was held at the Miatta Conference Hall in Freetown and included pastors from many countries.

Just over ten years after I had fully committed service to God, I experienced Him opening up more doors of ministry that I had not expected. Between 2001 and 2003, as a result of the Miatta Conference event, I had the opportunity to help coordinate a crusade at the national stadium, which held about 40,000 people. We planned a conference that would involve approximately 1,500 pastors meeting for five days each morning. In the evenings, the crusade was held. The conference was held in the morning at Sanctuary of Praise Church and the evening crusade services were held at the national stadium. Victory Christian Center sponsored the crusade. I had the opportunity to speak at both the pastors' conference and at the crusade. Approximately 40,000+ attended the crusade services each night and crowds also stood outside the stadium.

Since that time, God has continued to show me new opportunities for service to others. Perhaps most notably, the Lord orchestrated the intersection of my life with that of Mark Stewart. From the time Mark first invited me to get involved in 2002, my role progressed from leading the establishment of Hope Universal in Sierra Leone and Liberia to serving as Country Director, Regional Director, African Director and International Director.

Currently, I serve as a minister within the Bethel World Outreach Ministries, serve on their National Executive Council, represent Hope Universal, and serve as a missionary through the International Missionary Center. Through those roles, I facilitate church leader conferences, primarily through the International Missionary Center. In addition, I have the privilege of serving as a volunteer National Coordinator for Sierra Leone for Gideons International and serve as a board member of a Christian micro-finance institution named "A Call to Business." I look forward with faith to new opportunities to serve the Lord and the individuals and organizations that collaborate with us.

A considerable amount of time has passed since I made a commitment to the Lord in 1990. My circumstances have changed. I have aged physically and matured spiritually for more than two decades since I fervently prayed to survive so that I could fully serve.

As a young boy in Rivercess County, I never could have guessed what the Lord would do with my life. When we moved from the village to Monrovia, I experienced the excitement of seeing vehicles and tall buildings and staying with family members. As my education progressed through high school, I dreamed of a career in the medical field.

War affected all that I knew. As a result of that prayer under my bed in 1990, my whole way of thinking about life changed. Aspirations and plans are good but how the world looks can change at any time. The best thing anyone can do is to put all they have in the purpose of God. When I did that, I did not know how the Lord would work in my life, but He is faithful. He protected me and enabled me to not only survive, but to survive for purpose. The Lord spared my life. By His grace, I have no regrets. Even when I speak with acquaintances of mine who went on to become successful medical professionals in the U.S. and Europe, I am pleased with the path I have chosen.

Looking back, I realize that only by God's grace have I survived. Though times and circumstances have changed, my commitment to the Lord is new each day. My life is connected to His purpose. Looking forward, I am committed to serving the Lord for the rest of my days for His glory. My deepest desire is to serve Him with my life—to survive for *His* purpose.

AFTERWORD

September 10, 2014, Anderson, SC, USA

L ast evening, while in Anderson, SC, I reviewed some sections of this book prior to giving a presentation at the Anderson County Library. My mind was drawn to memories of lying under my bed in Monrovia, Liberia, in July 1990. As I reviewed that section of this book, I reflected on parallels between then and now. Though more than 24 years have passed, major challenges remain. In 1990, the threat was civil war, which not only materialized in Liberia but also spread to reach me and many others in Sierra Leone. In 2014, one of the major threats is the spread of Ebola, a deadly virus, the death toll of which continues to increase in both Liberia and Sierra Leone.

Ebola is not a bomb or a missile falling on buildings and houses; it's not the same as being killed by a machete. The result of its threat, however, is similar: fear. Ebola's dark shadow and the casualties within it are causing many to fear for life. One can hear gunfire and grenades, but Ebola is a silent killer, creeping through towns and villages familiar to me and taking lives of people I know. Like war, the spread of Ebola disrupts churches, schools, employment, and all other aspects of daily life.

Ebola emerges as another example of life's inevitable conflict. How do we handle conflict? How do we face what appears to be insurmountable difficulty and hardship? I am convinced that we look to God. God is faithful and by turning to Him again and again our faith becomes stronger. He delivers us, not necessarily from conflict, but from fear.

Much has changed in my life since 1990, since the outset of the war in Liberia and Sierra Leone. When I prayed to God for deliverance in 1990, I was not married and had no children. I had not seen the establishment of churches and schools. I had not worked in a medical clinic or led a pastor's conference. The stakes today seem higher. When I think about deliverance and survival, I immediately think not so much about myself but about my wife, my children, and the many individuals with whom I have developed relationships since 1990. I believe my faith must be even stronger now because so many others are involved.

When reflecting on the fearsome threats of war in 1990 and Ebola in 2014, I realize the essence of my story remains the same. Through faith in God we can overcome adversity—war or disease or any other calamity—regardless of the outcome. The Lord Jesus stated in John 16:33, "I have told you these things, so that in me you may have peace. In this world you will have trouble. But take heart! I have overcome the world" (NIV). We also read in Romans 8:28, "And we know that in all things God works for the good of those who love him, who have been called according to his purpose" (NIV). Those two verses convey how each of us—under the peace-giving love, guidance, and protection of God—can survive for purpose.

CPSIA information can be obtained
at www.ICGtesting.com
Printed in the USA
LVOW08*0231150617
538142LV00004B/10/P